'Situationist ideas have been trickling
for some time now. This book by Al
strate the relevance of these concepts
Ivan Chtcheglov and a whole host
make fresh connections. It is written with pathos and backed up by a wealth of academic and hard to come by radical texts. I find it a fascinating corrective to depoliticised takes on the Situationist Internationalists and I hope it inspires new research into the relationship between people and their environments.'

–Babak Fozooni, Associate Lecturer, The Open University, UK

'Alex Bridger's book brings together psychogeography and psychology in a challenge to conventional ways of undertaking academic work. The concepts from both academic fields are well-explained and, in a language accessible to anyone interested in either subject area, scholars or otherwise. Notably, this is a practice-based text, demonstrating the importance of actually carrying out the psychogeographical work in the field, with its socio-political significance well-situated in contemporary times. Bridger instils himself in the text via his practice, demonstrating the importance of the subjective aspect of psychogeography, one that, he explains, is problematic in his own academic field, psychology. It is this, he says, that is its "political purpose", and this too, is what makes the book so significant today. But it is also a personal project for Bridger, and this is what makes it readily available to any potentially interested reader. Bridger's book is both a new addition to the growing psychogeographical corpus, but also stands in its own right as an excellent current introduction to the subject.'

–Tina Richardson, author/editor of *Walking Inside Out: Contemporary British Psychogeography*

PSYCHOGEOGRAPHY AND PSYCHOLOGY

Psychogeography usually refers to radical and artistic ways of walking or to a conflation of psychology with geography. In this unique work, the author makes arguments for considering psychogeography as a way to critique the contemporary world and to consider new ways of studying the interface of human beings in environments.

The book begins by introducing and explaining the term *psychogeography* from a range of academic, activist, and artistic perspectives. Each chapter presents different approaches to doing psychogeography, and there are arguments presented for why there is a need for a postpsychology. The author takes a creative and innovative approach to psychogeography by extending walking methods of research to include other forms of practice and research including playwriting and wargaming.

The only book written on psychogeography from a psychological perspective, this book will appeal to researchers and students of psychology, geography, architecture, and cultural studies as well as artists, activists, and the public.

Alex Bridger is a Senior Lecturer in Critical Social Psychology at the University of Huddersfield. He is also one of the co-founders of the 4th World Congress of Psychogeography and is an active member of the trans-institutional Discourse Unit.

Concepts For Critical Psychology: Disciplinary Boundaries Re-Thought

Series editor: Ian Parker

Developments inside psychology that question the history of the discipline and the way it functions in society have led many psychologists to look outside the discipline for new ideas. This series draws on cutting edge critiques from just outside psychology in order to complement and question critical arguments emerging inside. The authors provide new perspectives on subjectivity from disciplinary debates and cultural phenomena adjacent to traditional studies of the individual.

The books in the series are useful for advanced level undergraduate and postgraduate students, researchers and lecturers in psychology and other related disciplines such as cultural studies, geography, literary theory, philosophy, psychotherapy, social work and sociology.

Most recently published titles:

The Event of Psychopoetics
Imagination and the Rupture of Psychology
Raúl García

Psychogeography and Psychology
In and Beyond the Discipline
Alex J. Bridger

PSYCHOGEOGRAPHY AND PSYCHOLOGY

In and Beyond the Discipline

To Elizabeth,

Hope you enjoy the book!

From Alex

Alex J. Bridger

Routledge
Taylor & Francis Group
LONDON AND NEW YORK

Cover image: Getty

First published 2022
by Routledge
4 Park Square, Milton Park, Abingdon, Oxon OX14 4RN

and by Routledge
605 Third Avenue, New York, NY 10158

Routledge is an imprint of the Taylor & Francis Group, an informa business

British Library Cataloguing-in-Publication Data
A catalogue record for this book is available from the British Library

Library of Congress Cataloging-in-Publication Data
A catalog record has been requested for this book

ISBN: 9781138124547 (hbk)
ISBN: 9781138124554 (pbk)
ISBN: 9781315648095 (ebk)

DOI: 10.4324/9781315648095

Typeset in Bembo
by Newgen Publishing UK

For Sam and Theo

CONTENTS

PREFACE

The discipline of psychology is very clear about how you should get from A to B, and it marks the journey from one point to the other through time and space, misdirecting us as it does so. Psychology's misunderstanding of the nature of space, of the geographical and architectural domains that enclose and define it, is modelled on its misunderstanding of time. This is through a simplistic causal relationship between things that are done to people, usually in the laboratory, and things that they do in response to that. The relationship between cause and effect that is then implemented in 'field' studies outside laboratories reduces human beings to objects, pushed and pulled in different directions, sometimes observed and measured by the researcher. Then their journey through space is conceived in the same kind of way; as if people follow a little cognitive map of the world inside their head, and go from point A, as if it were the origin and cause of their journey, to point B, the end point.

But a lot happens in between A and B that psychologists usually have not a clue about, and that is the real stuff of critical psychology, the stuff that is described and illuminated in this path-breaking book about 'psychogeography'. Alex J Bridger takes us out beyond the discipline, and into the real world, showing how our research must focus on the messy complicated journeys we take together around the world and on the collective experience of being in the world while we try to change it. This book opens out a whole new conceptual panorama, one that intersects with radical interventions in politics and culture and that takes us from the work of the Situationists decades ago to current psychogeographical forays into our fractured conflictual reality. The Situationists, remember, were concerned with a very different understanding of and relation to the world than what we find when we look at the importance of the 'situation' in our textbooks. The Situationists who are now one of the conceptual historical roots of psychogeography had their own international organisation, the Situationist International, and their intervention was directed at our place in global politics, a politics that is infused with semiotics – the meaning of things we encounter in the world – and action, how we always in some way replicate the shape of the world or disturb it while building something different together.

This book gives you an alternative history of the discipline of psychology, taking you on a journey into a parallel universe where people are agents, actively making and remaking the world, and it operates as a kind of handbook, helping you to navigate not only the existing discipline but also new spaces. This takes you into new space and prepares you to find space to do new work. The book claims in its subtitle, and it is quite right – it does what says on the tin – to be 'in' and 'beyond' the discipline. It is within the discipline, making sense of it as it notices what obstacles there are to doing good research, taking those obstacles seriously instead of merely taking them for granted. In that sense, it enacts in its account a 'psychogeographical' understanding of psychology. Psychology is treated as an institution that confines us and, as feminists have insisted when they speak of 'glass ceilings', we need to know something about the architecture, think about how it holds us in place as a kind of space that crystallises contemporary forms of power. And this book is 'beyond' the discipline, learning from the outsiders, it is 'outwith' psychology, a model of what critical psychology should be.

Ian Parker
University of Manchester

ACKNOWLEDGEMENTS

This book has taken a few years longer to complete than I had hoped! I am very thankful to the publishing and editorial team including Alex Howard, Eleanor Taylor, Hemalatha K and Akshita Patayani as well as the series editor Professor Ian Parker for enabling me to have a number of extensions for this book. The book is all the better for the extensions as it has allowed me to explore and expand into new dimensions of psychogeographical research such as playwriting and wargaming. The work here brings together ideas and arguments not only from my PhD thesis but also from recent published papers and book chapters that have been rewritten and expanded into a monograph format. I am thankful for the many discussions in recent years with fellow psychogeographers from academic, artistic and activist circles such as Tina Richardson, Tim Waters, Phil Wood, Graeme Murrell, Fiona Weir, Carl Meddings, David Smith, John Billingsley, Sophia Emmanouil and of course Charlotte Tillbury. Key supporters and allies also include Nigel King, Tim Gomersall and Surya Munro. Big thanks out to Darrin Hodgetts, Kerry Chamberlain, Paula Reavey and Geoff Bunn for their advice and guidance in writing about psychogeography for academic audiences. I should also mention that LGBTQ+ psychogeography project discussed in Chapter 3 was made possible via funding from the British Academy/Leverhulme. My cat Emily also helped with the production of this book, and she is a true psychogeographer and flâneuse.

1

INTRODUCTION TO PSYCHOGEOGRAPHY

Not many people would identify themselves as psychogeographers and even less so as psychogeographical psychologists. However, the practice of psychogeography is something that many of us already do without naming it as psychogeography or as psychogeographical. For example, we might choose to walk or drive down a different road or path, or we may get off the bus at a stop earlier than our designated one and we might more consciously take in and experience our surrounding environments and try to make sense of and critique how things are. We might wonder what lay before a demolished building and what will go in its place and whether it will be another new supermarket or something else. We might consider how environments make us feel and we might consider what a place looks like if it was not based purely on consumerist values. In the online world, we might choose to do a psychogeographical wander by seeing where one random web link takes us via the Google search engine. These are some practices that psychogeographers do. Many of those familiar with the idea of psychogeography might associate it with the situationist practice of the dérive, which refers to a radical way to wander around urban environments to critique the capitalist formation of spaces and places. It is therefore a way of not simply going from A to B and re-explaining what we see and think, but rather it is a practice of taking ourselves beyond the usual ways in how we do things or think about things to begin to see things from new and possibly more critical perspectives. One example widely used by writers of psychogeography

DOI: 10.4324/9781315648095-1

(i.e. Richardson, 2015) to explain what psychogeography means is to pick up a map of somewhere that you would like to go to and then to work out a route from one destination to another. However, rather than using that map to get from A to B, you would have to use another map to get from A to B with the overarching aim to lose a sense of place in order to be more open to environmental effects rather than to use the map as a means of orientating oneself. Why should we deliberately aim to disorientate ourselves? This should be asked in relation to the present neoliberal order of things and with respect to what this contributes to extending critical psychology research. These are questions that I now turn to and consider.

In the present context, we are faced with the continuation of austerity measures, the spectre of terrorism, what outcomes the UK's Brexit vote will lead to, the rise of the coronavirus disease (COVID-19) and also the turn by many people to voting for right wing political parties and the rise of populism. One would think that amidst this scenario that neoliberalism would be in crisis and that people would be turning to Left wing and 'critical' alternatives, but this does not seem to have been the case, at least in countries such as the United Kingdom, the United States of America and across Europe. Indeed, there is currently quite an anti-intellectual climate and there is thus more favour and support for populist voices such as the ex-US President Donald Trump, the current UK Prime Minister Boris Johnson and the popularity of non-expert voices. Arguably then, there is a narrowing of position from showcasing a range of voices and perspectives in the mass media to just presenting a few dominant and mainstream voices, i.e. right wing, pro-Brexit and nationalist voices. Let me demonstrate this particular argument by focusing on the UK general election of 2019 and by linking this example to discursive and psychogeographical approaches. In order to get to what a psychogeographical approach can do and what it might mean in a critical psychological context, I need to begin with methods familiar to critical psychologists and readers new to this approach via Parker's approach (1996) to discourse analysis. I begin with the position that 'discourses' are 'sets of statements that construct objects and subject positions' (Parker, 1994, 245). I have chosen discourse analysis here because of the focus on relations of power as opposed to studying relations of meaning and because of key concepts that I consider as relevant and useful, which include discourses, rhetoric (how language is used and what language does), subject positions (who speaks and who do they speak for), institutions and power (relations of power and not relations of meaning) and finally subjectivity (relations between readers and the text). From that approach, I will introduce a brief psychogeographical analysis and will consider the importance of spatialising discourses and what such an approach can offer to critical psychologists. The following analysis also serves as a further way to explain one psychogeographical way of understanding and critiquing the social world.

During the U.K. general election of 2019, the Conservative Party ran with the moto 'Get Brexit Done', and in various interviews with its leader, Boris Johnson repeated the statement without adding anything to further that plan. Brexit was seen to be a 'natural' order of things, and it was viewed by the government as 'the will of the people', even though only 52% of the people in the country voted for Brexit and even with the rationale for Brexit still being largely unclear. In British newspapers, in social media and on television, the moto of 'Get Brexit Done' by the Conservative leader was accompanied by various mass media reports such as Johnson driving a JCB Military Backhoe Loader through a white brick wall (www.youtube.com/watch?v=4PYU5q1RJv4).

The choice of vehicle here is important given JCB's connection with the UK's Ministry of Defence and with providing militarised vehicles for theatres of war worldwide. Moreover, Johnson received a £1210,000 donation from the Chairman of JCB, Anthony Bamford (Lockley, 2019). On the JCB's YouTube site, the Military Backhoe Loader is presented as a fast, aggressive and resilient vehicle. Particular words are used to describe the JCB, which include 'MOBILITY, PERFORMANCE, PROTECTION' (JCB, 2019). The vehicle has been designed to provide support for armed forces in order to build trenches, to clear obstacles and to create firing positions. The vehicle also has some armoured protection (Military Today, 2021). It is an unfortunate choice of vehicle to use, given the use of JBC vehicles to bulldoze settlements on Palestinian land (Nieuwhof, 2018). The choice of vehicle by Johnson and the Conservatives is therefore important to the context of Brexit in that it can be represented in the context of war rhetoric. Such representations can be said to map onto other wider social discourses and media texts such as the film *Brexit: An Uncivil War* and also to World War II and the United Kingdom and its Allies against Hitler and the Nazis. Indeed, it seems that Johnson models himself on statesmen such as Churchill, and this is often exemplified in the stylisation of his speeches and how he presents himself to the world's media. For example, one can see how he presents himself as a statesman in relation to recent government announcements about COVID-19 in various news briefings. In one recent video circulated via various UK news outlets, Johnson drives a JCB through a 'gridlock' wall (On Demand News, 2019). The camera focuses initially on a wall titled as 'GRIDLOCK'. Then a crashing sound is heard and the JCB crashes through the wall with a placard of 'Get Brexit Done' on the front of the bulldozer attachment. The driver is Prime Minister Boris Johnson. He then slows the vehicle to a stop, exits and poses for the cameras briefly. He then walks around the gallery of farming vehicles.

The start of the video clip is particularly interesting in that it begins with a shot of a white brick wall with the wording of 'GRIDLOCK' in big red chunky letters in the centre of the image. The red text is very clear to read against the backdrop of the white brick wall. The choice of red font may confer a sense of emergency. The gridlock is arguably meant to represent the situation in Parliament back in November 2019, whereby attempts by the Conservative Party to get their Brexit policies through Parliament were repeatedly blocked by members of its own Party and of the other Parties (i.e. Labour, Liberals, Greens and Plaid Cymru). Interestingly, after the Conservative Party won the General Election in late 2019, many UK news commentators spoke about the Party breaking through the 'Red Wall' in the North of England and of taking Labour seats. On watching the video clip further, a few seconds later, the sound of the vehicle can be heard, and then shortly afterwards, something can begin to be seen crashing through the wall at some speed. The polystyrene bricks crash to the floor. Then becomes visible the text of 'Get Brexit Done' in white font on a dark blue background. This represents the outcome of an 'aggressive' Brexit strategy by the Conservative Party to 'get Brexit done'. The dark blue background of the text looks to be the same as the colour scheme of the Conservative Party. The Conservative Party is arguably responsible for getting Brexit done. The white text on blue background is also clear to read. Beyond the text, we see that the placard is carried within a JCB with a bulldozer attachment. In between the bulldozer attachment and the driver window is displayed the British flag. Johnson is seen sitting in the JCB looking very happy with himself and behind him is a person also sitting down in the vehicle. Presumably the other person is lending support in terms of driving the vehicle safely. The video clip is only approximately 12 seconds in duration and then is repeated but this time from a side camera view, where one can see the moto from a side-angle view and also the JCB arms with the logo of the sales and hire company 'Trucks R Us'. The side view show of the video also indicates that the JCB is fully emblazoned across the whole vehicle with the British flag, right from the wheel across to the panels and arms. Johnson drives the vehicle a few metres further, stops and then gets out. He poses for the cameras briefly on exiting the vehicle, then climbs down the JCB steps and walks around the vehicle. He pauses briefly by the side of the bulldozer attachment and gives a double thumbs up to the cameras. He has only three words to say to the journalists, which is unsurprisingly, 'Get Brexit Done', and then he walks away through what appears to be a photographic gallery of farming vehicles.

A simple account of the video would merely re-explain the context of what happened and what the video means for the strategy of getting Brexit done and thus would not really be any different to a journalistic account. However, a critical psychological and qualitative discourse analysis of the video yields much more detailed interpretation. A critical discursive approach enables us to deconstruct the video image and text as well as to present the dominant visual and textual discourses to explain how those discourses map onto wider discourses in society. The mantra of 'Get Brexit Done' makes sense in the context of 'Brexit means Brexit' because it is a simple and literal 'thing', which will be made possible and thus serves as an effective interpretative repertoire here. It is at this point that it is possible to begin thinking about the video from a psychogeographical psychological standpoint in considering the spatialising of the discourses in the video and to consider the environment presented. In the video, Johnson drives the JCB in a straight line through the brick wall. The solution to Brexit appears as a clear and simple path from A to B with Johnson in the driving seat leading the strategy. The JCB crashing through the wall is akin to a military leader leading the charge against its enemies – presumably the anti-Brexiteers and anyone else from other political parties that didn't support the Conservative policy on Brexit. We have here, Johnson driving the JCB, which we also know is modified to be used as a military vehicle in theatres of war, as discussed earlier on in this chapter. He drives the JCB but could equally have been presented as a war leader such as Duke Wellington on a horse charging against the enemy. The video thus abounds with a rhetoric of war, whereby Johnson positions himself as a statesman of sorts, albeit this time, the general in a JCB vehicle rather than on a horse or in a tank. Now I will present a short summary of the discourse analysis and then will explain how we can use the findings to inform what a psychogeographical approach might begin to look like. The brief analysis has drawn on Parker's (1994) approach to discourse analysis. The key discourses produced include 'Get Brexit done', i.e. Brexit as the 'will of the people' and a military discourse, i.e. Brexit as akin to a war struggle. The second concept is that of rhetoric. Here war rhetoric is deployed to describe a solution to the Brexit 'gridlock' as well as to represent a militarised version of a JCB vehicle. The subject positions include Johnson as leading the charge against Brexit, Johnson as statesman and Johnson as leader. He metaphorically utilises the machinery of Brexit to get it done, i.e. Johnson driving the JCB and leading the charge into the Brexit 'gridlock'. The JCB represents the aggressiveness and ability to get Brexit done. The next concept is that of institutions and power, whereby the Conservative Party can be construed as the party of business and the only party that can enact the change required to get through the Brexit 'gridlock'. The next concept is that of subjectivity where this relates to the 'viewers' as audience and my position on the Left. This position has informed my reading of this set of video images. The final concept is that of the dilemma as Brexit. The argument posited by Johnson is that Brexit must get done as things are gridlocked and change is not possible and therefore Johnson and the Conservative Party are the only 'solution' to get Brexit done. Here then is a brief Parkerian discourse analysis of the video and now follows a short psychogeographical reflection on that work. It is possible to consider the discourse analysis of the video previously in relation to considering spatialisation of these discourses. There can be no simple solution to Brexit. There is no 'straight line' from gridlock to a solution to Brexit. What needs to be done is to point to possible alternative solutions and to consider alternatives to a neoliberal solution to Brexit.

The previous discourse and psychogeographical readings of the video hopefully begin to enable readers of this book to become more acquainted with what a psychogeographical approach to critical psychological research might begin to look like. Next, I continue with the theme of the current social context of how things are and from there will then discuss previous academic literature from social psychology, environmental psychology, human geography and political theory.

For many people in contemporary society, the idea of Left-wing governments with their manifestos for change seems out of reach. Many television shows and films fantasise about impending apocalypses, zombie outbreaks and how we could improve our homes and live happier and healthier lives by eating more healthily and taking more active pursuits. In a neoliberal order of things, change has to come from 'within' the person and threats to the established order of things come from outside the person and from other groups such as the anarchists, the communists and the terrorists. If people are unhappy with their lives and how things are, then they simply have to change their job, their house, their relationships and what they wear. Readers may be familiar with homemaking programmes such as *The Perfect Home* and *Grand Designs*, which encourage its viewers to think about how different types of homes make us feel and to think about what ideal living environments could look like. Whilst such programmes might be useful to think about how we might go about improving our homes, they also stop short of thinking about how we might go about changing society. The neoliberal order of things is thus beyond criticism, presented as a perfect ordering of society and as such is an ideological constellation, a particular way of understanding oneself in the world, a way in which one can navigate in a straight-line life's trajectory from birth to death. Living in a neoliberal way is a less complicated, less conflictual and easier path to traverse. However, being critical of the neoliberal order of things is arguably a different, albeit more critical and balanced way in which one can be patriotic. Billig (1995) explains in his book *Banal Nationalism* that patriotism can be a form of nationalism. The question here I would like to present is, why couldn't there be better alternatives to the current neoliberal order of things? Why should we have to settle with a neoliberal order of things where there are vast inequalities between the rich and the poor, where the richest countries of the world have growing numbers of food bank users and with the capitalist dream where one can only be successful if one works hard enough? What could a psychogeographical approach do in terms of providing a critique of neoliberalism and with paving ways forward for a new order of things? In presenting answers to these questions, it is important first of all to conceptualise what a psychogeographical psychological approach could look like, what the key concepts are and then to conclude with what the implications of such an approach could be for considering social change and a possible world beyond neoliberalism.

Mainstream psychologists (i.e. cognitive, evolutionary and behaviourist) have tended to shy away from questions about politics and what implications their research has to society and various institutions and groups. However, one of the premises of some qualitative researchers including the Feminists, Marxists and radical psychologists has been to keep politics and their reflective positions at the forefront of their work. In terms of taking a position as a critical psychologist and being involved with this book series, I take seriously the notion of reflexivity and with considering the relations of my work to society. In order to establish the key concepts for a psychogeographical psychological approach, it is important first of all to set out my reflective approach to this research and from what position I begin from. Given that I am talking here about psychogeographical approach, it is useful to start with a beginning of sorts and what led me into psychogeography. This could be useful for readers to trace the route that I have taken from critical psychology and Foucauldian discourse analysis in order to get to psychogeography.

In my early days as a PhD student at the Discourse Unit at Manchester Metropolitan University, I read Sadie Plant's (1992) book *The Most Radical Gesture: The Situationist International in the Post-Modern Age*, and this led me to various fanzines, books and articles about the situationists. This was a book that my then supervisor, Professor Ian Parker, had recommended to me. I think he suggested the book to me because I had spoken about visiting the Communist Museum in Prague and how I had found it strange that the historical artefacts of that time were exhibited in glass cabinets. We spoke in supervision about the conception of recuperation and how dominant groups in society shape political and social narratives of each epoch in history. At the time, I was also exploring Left-wing political theories and I was particularly interested in the work of the situationists and how they had managed to write in various mediums including full intellectual prose as well as film making, art and photography. Most people would generally equate the situationists with the practice of psychogeographical walking, but this was only one phase of their work that took place for a few years from the late 1950s to the early 1960s. Later in this book, I will cover more recent aspects of their work and how this applies to what I do as a psychogeographical psychologist, mainly in terms of psychogeographical wargaming and in terms of developing a psychogeographical psychological approach.

In 2001, I was working on my PhD about the events of September 11th and the aftermath and was doing discursive and situationist analyses of word and image news reports and images of the World Trade Centre attacks and responses from political leaders from Bin Laden to Bush. I began my academic studies in psychology with an interest in discourse analysis and how the concepts could be used to deconstruct the dominant order of things in the world. Discourse analysis is a very useful approach in which to deconstruct dominant discourses and to take apart what is presented by political leaders and the mass media as natural, true and real. I had started my research by using a discursive approach to deconstruct dominant representations of September 11th and the aftermath, and this then led me to consider how to go about studying and experiencing the physical space of Ground Zero. There were not really any existing methods or approaches in psychology at the time that would enable me to do that, and I was also keen to explore how a situationist approach to psychography could be deployed in a qualitative way. This led me to consider the practice of psychogeography and to their critical political analysis of environments. Situationist psychogeography does not originate from academia and neither would any of its proponents argue that it should be located there. However, as a critical intellectual, artistic and politically based approach, it has value for those wishing to take critical approaches in academia (i.e. critical psychology) as well as those based in activist groups and for anyone else striving towards radical social change. Later in this book, I will discuss initial psychogeographical research that I undertook at Ground Zero in New York. For now, I need to turn back to the rationale for a psychogeographical approach and to continue with a review of the literature that sets the concepts and foundations for this critical psychological approach.

Given that psychogeography is still not an established approach in psychology, it is necessary to forge new concepts for what such an approach can look like. I take seriously the importance of concepts and theory in one's research, and for that reason, the psychogeographical concepts and theory are bound up with my reflective approach. Ontology is thus important as the concepts are what bind together my unique approach as a psychogeographer and as a critical psychologist. My specific interest in psychogeography stems from my curiosity in understanding environments, with a Left-wing position and with considering alternative ways of understanding and critiquing the social order of things. My Left-wing position informs my approach to academic work. However, one does not have to be Left wing or have a political position to practice psychogeography. Academic work is however quite sedentary and involves sitting down for long periods of time. The practice of psychogeography can be rather different in that it can involve movement and as such there can be many positive health benefits. Many of those familiar with the term *psychogeography* would associate it with walking, but this is actually quite a limited way to understand the approach. What I want to do in this book is to present an expanded notion of psychogeography, which moves beyond viewing it as simply an approach of 'critical' walking and instead understanding that it can also be a philosophical approach to the world and a way to spatially deconstruct the order of things whether this be via walking, thinking or other means.

Some readers of this book may have the view that psychogeography is basically just a conflation of psychology with geography and that would not be a mistaken point of view. In the area of academic psychology, the term *psychogeography* originates in journals such *Environmental Psychology*, where the term was used in the 1980s to refer to an interface between psychology and geography, and to the study of effects between the human mind and environments (Wood, 1987). In more recent years, such arguments have been connected to the psychological study of spaces and places (Moser and Uzzell, 2003), how environments causally effect behaviours and to the study of societal and social processes (Gifford, 2014). Many such researchers have attempted to study spaces and places as seemingly neutral containers of meaning bereft of any consideration of politics, economics and also social and cultural issues (Spink and Spink, 2015). Seemingly, the focus has only been on individual cognitions and behaviour and considering environmental 'variables' such as heat, light and noise (Harris et al., 2002). Wider social contextual frameworks such as neoliberalism and consumer citizenship are incredibly difficult things to 'measure' and beyond the methodological focus of cognitive experimental psychological research.

However, I don't wish to simply make a case for psychogeography merely being a conflation of geography and psychology as it can be much more than that as will be explained in the remainder of this chapter. What I want to do here is to lay out arguments for a psychogeographical psychological approach that is attuned to a political purpose and which makes connections not only to other disciplines including critical psychology but also to human geography and arts-based research. In the position that I take as a psychogeographer and critical psychologist, I see it as highly important to consider the political and social implications of research, and for this reason, my approach to psychogeography is rather different from that of the classic environmental psychologists, geographers and place-based identity psychology researchers. Next in this chapter, a review of literature within traditional and contemporary fields of research from psychology, geography, politics and situationist theory will be considered.

Within sub-disciplinary areas of psychology including social psychology and environmental psychology, key topics of study have included place identity, group conflict and the contact hypothesis. In that work, researchers have studied how people relate to places and spaces and how environments can lead to the construction of new social and personal identities. Much of that work has been important in aiming to reduce social conflict between people and for fostering more positive relations between different communities. In this chapter, I will expand further on key aspects of that work. The work of Altman (1993) is important to begin with here. Altman argued that human relationships are contextualised in what he refers to as activity settings. In specific settings, people draw on behaviours that are deemed as normal to those contexts. It would, for example, be perceived as normative behaviour to wait in line in a queue in a coffee shop to order a coffee, but it would not be normal to go back to the end of the queue after waiting to order a coffee. This particular scenario actually took place at a psychogeography festival and conference in June 2008, the *Territories Reimagined: International Perspectives* conference and festival. Such actions thus bring to light what can be deemed as normative and non-normative behaviours. What I want to do here is to extend the arguments to consider other formations of identity and behaviour in places and spaces, and so now it is necessary to turn to the work of other researchers such as Cuba and Hummon (1993). Place identity research in social psychology and environmental psychology on the study of place are key areas of research to consider in relation to considering the formation of a psychogeographical psychological approach. How we define whom we are is often bound up with a sense of place and in the context of groups that we may feel a part of. Cuba and Hummon (1993, 112) explain that, 'Like people, things and activities, places are an integral part of the social world of everyday life, as such, they become important mechanisms through which identity is defined and situated'. Indeed, when people make associations of place, they often also bind this together with particular memories (Cuba and Hummon, 1993), and then when we are in particular places, we then create and form new identities (Twigger-Ross and Uzzell, 1996). Manzo (2003) makes the case that we can often find ourselves 'out of place'. In Godfrey Reggio's film (1982), *Koyaanisqatsi*, the central meaning of the film is the notion that 'life is out of balance'. The study of identity is therefore important to how we might go about understanding ourselves, others and our place in the world. However, Durrheim and Dixon (2005, 180) quite rightly explain that places shouldn't just be viewed as 'inert backdrops to social relations'. Hodgetts et al. (2010, 287) explain that places and spaces should not be viewed simply as 'backdrops to social processes'. Taking a discursive point of view into consideration, Billig et al. (1988) state that the ways in which people identify with places are inherently dilemmatic. Any consideration of identity as situated in places should then be considered in terms of an explicit political analysis and with regard to the context of social processes and political change. These studies then also point to key limits with some of the existing cognitive experimental research with the assumptions of environments as simply being 'backdrops' or factors impacting on social processes and relationships. The arguments that Billig et al. (1988) raise are important in considering how people use language to talk about their identifications with place.

It is now necessary to turn to the contact hypothesis as conceptualised by Allport (1954). His work was key in terms of leading many social psychologists to the question of how to reduce conflict between people and in order to increase harmonious relations between people. Contact between different people and groups is crucial. Nowell et al. (2006) explain that when people perceive positive connections with places, then the likelihood of people participating in their local communities will be greater. The ethos then of intergroup conflict work as well as work in the areas of place identity and activity settings is therefore most useful in terms of attempting to reduce conflict between people in society. However, the notion of community is a very amorphous term, and it is important to consider whose 'community' we are talking about. Furthermore, what I want to argue for here is to focus out from considering conflict between groups to considering the conflictual basis of neoliberalism and consumer society. A political focus of research is a stance not adopted by many traditional and cognitive experimental social psychologists though it is a stance that is key in the approach advocated in this book. In disciplines such as human geography and critical psychology, notions of politics, power and ideology are at the forefront of some peoples' research. For example, Keith and Pile (1993) explain that the focus on place identity research must be linked to the study of power and ideology. In a discourse analytic study by Dixon and Durrheim (2000), they discuss problematic social relations between black and white people at a coastal resort in KwaZulu Natal, South Africa. In that study, they found that desegregation changed the relations between people and that the then dominant group, i.e. the white people, actively resisted and opposed black people using the same social spaces as them. Reading such accounts seems alarming by today's standards, but back then, such perceptions were considered as 'normal'. It is thus crucial to conduct research to call into question such normalised perceptions and discourses of race, culture and groups, and this is where concepts such as interpretative repertoires are of great importance in order to critique taken for granted accounts that normalise racist ways of thinking and behaving. However, it is useful to not only consider peoples' language but also study everyday life itself. Other writers have argued that social psychological research has focused too much on place identities (Dixon and Durrheim, 2000). Further questioning could be considered in relation to spaces and places, which might serve to normalise certain ways of thinking and being. These questions then lead us into other disciplinary modes of inquiry, which include sociology, urban studies and human geography. I begin next with the work of Merrifield. Merrifield (1993, 522) explains that places are where 'everyday life is situated'. His argument makes it all the more important to analyse and critique everyday spaces and places. Merrifield (1993) goes further in his thesis and indicates that environments should not be seen simply as blank tabula rasa onto which meanings can be written but rather that it is necessary to think about how such places are written onto via various capitalist, consumerist and commercialist institutions and groups and that this in turn has the effect of shaping peoples' experiences. Indeed, Lefebvre (1976, 21) argues that:

> What has happened is that capitalism has found itself able to attenuate (if not resolve) its internal contradictions for a century, and consequently, in the hundred years since the writings of *Capital*, it has succeeded in achieving 'growth'. We cannot calculate at what price, but we do know the means: *by occupying space, by producing a space*.

A key question here to consider is where has psychological research made sense of how capitalism has shaped peoples' everyday lives, their perceptions of themselves, their relations with others and social systems and structures in society? These are questions that have only begun to be considered in recent years by critical psychologists and psychologists positioning themselves on the Left or as Marxist, Feminist or community social psychologists. Experimental social psychological research on place has enforced European–American ideas of individualism and capitalist achievement (Corral-Verdugo and Pinheiro, 2009). If we want to study peoples' experiences of places, then it is important to locate such accounts in a proper social, cultural and historical context and to explore how such accounts are enmeshed within discourses of 'capitalism, rationalism, modernisation, the Puritan work ethic and spectacle' (Sadler, 1998/1999, 96). Sadler (1998/1999, 96) argued that individuals' experiences of places are enmeshed within wider discourses of 'capitalism, rationalism, modernisation, the Puritan work ethic and the spectacle'. There are indeed many recent examples where individuals have challenged the dominant order of things in relation to consumer capitalism and democracy to occupations of space in Tahir Square, Zuccotti Park and London (Žižek, 2011).

Psychological research can therefore be extended by considering the impacts of neoliberalism and consumerism upon peoples' everyday experiences of the world and by encouraging such reflections to build greater awareness of current social conditions in order to generate new avenues for action and change. Moreover, how people use space is a question that has only recently been considered by social psychologists and environmental psychologists, but the focus has not been on a political analysis of uses of spaces or in how occupying spaces enables people to produce new spaces. This is where it is important to draw connections to political and urban theorists. Lefebvre (1976) argues for the importance of politically interpreting spaces and places. However, it is reassuring to find that there are some contemporary psychologists conducting social, community and health-based research that take such arguments seriously (Hodgetts et al., 2010). What I think is useful here is to consider the current social and political ordering of spaces and places in contemporary Western society. In order to answer that question, it is important to consider social spaces as consumer spaces. Pinder (1996, 414) argues for the need to study the 'social organisation of place' in order to understand how places produce meanings and to consider alternatives to the capitalist order of things. Stephen Miles (2010, 8), a cultural geographer and sociologist, indicates that consumerism is a 'thoroughly cultural phenomenon that serves to legitimate capitalism on an everyday basis'. If consumerism has such an 'effect' on peoples' lives, then why would we not study such effects? The effects of the environment on human minds is a key aspect of social psychological and environmental psychological research though what can be argued here is to consider the notion of effects in quite a different manner from that of the cognitive experimental psychologists. The notion of effects can thus be taken out of a causal and mechanist context of cognitive experimental research and instead should be applied to a discursive Foucauldian approach in considering the implications of language and what conditions of possibility are set up by a consumerist ordering of spaces and place in contemporary societies. This can also lead us to the notion of consumerism in relation to the work of Foucault and Focauldian scholars and their work on power relations and spatiality. The study of relations of power in places and spaces is arguably of central importance in doing psychogeographical work. My own approach as a critical psychologist has been greatly informed by Foucauldian discourse analysis and the attention to the study of relations of power as opposed to studying relations of meaning as with phenomenological research. In Foucault's (1967, 24) later work, he turned to two key concepts that he referred to as utopias and heterotopias. Utopias refers to what perfect imagined spaces and places could look like, but which were not actually real. Heterotopias refers to utopias that are realised spaces and places and which he refers to as 'effectively enacted utopia' (Foucault, 1967, 3). It is useful here to extend Foucault's analysis of places and spaces to contemporary consumer spaces such as shopping centres. At first thought, one may think initially that a shopping centre is just somewhere where people generally tend to indulge in a bit of carefree shopping. However, if one considers this example within a Foucauldian framework, then such spaces are not just about shopping but are also subject to surveillance and observation (Voyce, 2006). Hook's work (2007, 205) is particularly salient to discuss here as he writes about gated communities in South Africa and how 'spacialisation' is a 'means of meaning making and power' and that 'historical structures of privilege and exclusion are continually reproduced'. Davis and Monk (2008) also point to how spaces can be used as a disciplinary way to classify, police and control populations including various groups such as refugees and those with mental health needs. They also explain that 'the spatial logic of neoliberalism revives the most extreme colonial patterns of residential segregation and zoned consumption' (Davis and Monk, 2008, 15). Such arguments can then lead to the question of what to do about forms of governance that institute 'colonial patterns of residential segregation and zoned consumption' (Davis and Monk, 2008, 15). This then leads us to considering consumer capitalism further as will now be discussed in this chapter.

One of the key problems with mainstream social psychological and environmental psychology research has been the unquestioning acceptance of the consumer capitalist order of things and the 'failure to acknowledge the social embeddedness and emplacement of subjective experience and the power relations inherent in these dominant institutions' (McDonald et al., 2017). There is a need to produce non-commodified forms of academic knowledge in order to call into question the neoliberal order of things (McDonald et al., 2017). Mainstream environmental and social psychologists have not really undertaken political analyses of spaces and places. This is problematic given that consumer capitalist ideas do inform the design, form and function of urban spaces (Lefebvre, 1991; Miles, 2010, 2012; Peck and Tickell, 2002). Places such as shopping centres, airport shopping areas and theatres have become completely commodified spaces, which are structured to 'serve the calculative needs of money which … prioritises modes of interaction through exchange' (Miles, 2010, 17). The tourism industry is an interesting example here in relation to cultural icons, history and heritage that have become part of a new urban spectacle to be consumed by tourists and visitors. Objects of consumption can typically include merchandise and souvenirs (Gotham, 2002). Moreover, in recent years, there are examples where websites such as Airbnb advertise holidays in terms of the experiences that can be gained rather than simply as places to visit. Indeed, the types of interactions that human beings have with social spaces is based on 'relationships between individualised consumers and a market detached from local physical space' (Voyce, 2006, 274). Many public spaces have been turned into privatised spaces, which actively encourage consumer spending (Voyce, 2006). There is also an emotionality to such spaces as Miles (2012) argues, and this can be connected to the argument of psychologisation in relation to spaces and places. Though with the emotionality connection comes with it an increased alienation of people from each other and to places and spaces (Miles, 2012; Simmel, 1950). Giddens (1991, 242) discusses this in terms of 'disembeddedness', which he refers to as 'the lifting out of social relationships from local contexts and their recombination across indefinite time/space distances'. Manzo (2003) also discusses how people feel at the same time 'emplaced' and 'out of place'. Hodgetts, Stolte, et al. (2010) discuss how people who are homeless have been increasingly 'emplaced' in towns and cities in which they reside. This then leads to the question of how would people not feel emplaced and what would it take for people to feel situated in places and to feel comfortable, healthy and happy? The answer to this question comes in the form of consumer citizenship. Citizenship is not a fixed term, and in its current form, it can be considered as something that is tied to consumerism, and thus as consumer citizenship. Consumer citizenship has come to be accepted by many as who we are and how we form our identities within Western societies. Thus, the citizen as consumer is assumed to be self-governing, responsible and independent and whose life revolves around a connection to the free market and to enterprise. Those citizens who do not engage with such an ethic can become targeted as not responsible and not able to manage their own risks. Such citizens can then subsequently be excluded from society (Miles, 2012; Voyce, 2006) and within that demographic can include those with mental health needs, the homeless, the disabled and loitering groups of people who are invariably young people (Voyce, 2006). The modern Western focus on home ownership is also worthy of discussion here in terms of the cultural capital that it bestows on those who own property and land, i.e. the middle to upper classes. Though this in itself also creates difficulties for those who may struggle to access opportunities and resources (Mandipour, 2004). I am making a case here for doing research not just to simply reaffirm and legitimatise consumer culture and neoliberalism, but which can work to create alternative and potentially counter forms of academic knowledge. I take heed of arguments by writers such as Vail (2010, 312–313) that it is necessary to:

> Promote democratic control over the market … that are politically and socially embedded and grounded in a logic predicated on social needs rather than profit. It would include efforts to undermine the grip of market hegemony by increasing the transparency of the market and revealing its true social costs and consequences.

Psychologists working within the cognitive experimental scientific mode of inquiry have for too long neglected any consideration of the formation and use of spaces in relation to historical and social processes of change. I ally myself with other critical psychologists who argue that psychological work needs to be created to make knowledge that challenges the dominant neoliberal status quo (i.e. Hayes, 2003; Hook, 2007). Mainstream psychological work has all too often been co-opted by advertisers and consumer corporations to sell objects back to people and to fill their empty selves (Cushman, 1990). Arguably then, there is a need to develop new approaches and methods to critique the consumerisation of the social world and how we experience, we make sense of and to be critical of such spaces and places and the organisation of the social world.

At this point in the chapter, it is important to consider what previous existing critical psychology, human geography and political theory can be drawn on to begin to consider the context in which a psychogeographical approach could be forged. There is a sedentary focus on current psychological research (Sheller and Urry, 2006). What I argue for here is for *a spatial turn to place in psychology* (Bridger et al., 2019), which requires drawing on concepts and ideas from geography (Pinder, 1996), radical urban theory (Sadler, 1998/1999) and critical psychology (Burnett et al., 2004). There have been arguments in recent years for a 'new mobilities paradigm' (Sheller and Urry, 2006), which involves the study of peoples' experiences of movement. Arguably then, mobility should be viewed as a central feature of how everyday life occurs (Binnie et al., 2007). Radley et al. (2010) explains that people create lived-in accounts of experience in specific contexts and the idea of how we move from place to place continuously. Edensor (2008, 136–137) explains that, 'walking is suffused with a kaleidoscope of intermingling thoughts, experiences and sensations, so that the character of the walk is constantly shifting'. Other writers such as Sotelo (2010, 61) discuss the idea of 'participation cartography' and views walking not as a spatial process but rather as a 'performance of self in spatio-temporal terms'. In drawing on a methodology to study spaces and places, it is important to consider a full range of human perceptions including visual, auditory, embodied and sensory. It is useful to develop methods to study the visual world (Hodgetts et al., 2007) and to conceptualise visual analytic methods of research (Lykes et al., 2003; Pink, 2004).

One should consider what methods other researchers have used in relation to studying places and spaces and this has included go-along methods where researchers walk alongside participants and conduct interviews (Kusenbach, 2003), the practice of 'bimbling', which refers to walking at a leisurely pace (Anderson, 2004), and psychogeographical psychological wandering (Bridger, 2010, 2011, 2015). The three methods listed above will be elaborated further in Chapter 3 where I will talk about key vignettes from my own research practice. Sheller and Urry (2000) point to the sedentary nature of much of current applied social psychological research methods, and indeed there is scant work that explains how to use walking to document peoples' experiences (Sheller and Urry, 2006). In this book, arguments are made for the development of mobile methods and for a 'new mobilities paradigm' (Sheller and Urry, 2006, 207) with colleagues Brown and Durrheim (2009, 216) arguing that knowledge is 'constructed in and through mobile interactivity'. Particular types of mobile methods of research include work on photo elicitation methods and walking interviews and walking methods (Radley et al., 2010; Hodgetts et al., 2010). A psychogeographical psychological approach can connect with the sort of work done in the arena of 'mobile methods' (Sheller and Urry, 2006). Qualitative, health and critical social psychologists have argued that drawing on approaches such as walking can be a useful way to study spaces and places (Chamberlain, 2011; Hodgetts et al., 2010; Bridger, 2014). Moving through spaces and places is arguably a way to make sense of environments. However, one needs to be careful in not assuming that such work can get us closer to how things really are what things really mean. There is scant work in critical psychology with a psychogeographical focus, though it is that work that will be turned to in Chapter 2. In Chapter 2, I will begin in discussing the lineage of psychogeographical research from the early work of those such as Baudelaire and Engels, through to the work of the Surrealists, the Situationists, 'academic' psychogeography and then to the work of new psychogeographers and groups. To conclude this chapter, I present the following key points of summary, which include:

- Pointing to the limits of previous psychological research on spaces and places, i.e. depoliticisation and apolitical.
- Arguments for a *spatial turn in psychology*, considering social spaces as consumer spaces and a critique of the neoliberal order of things.
- Conceptualising a psychogeographical approach and methodology.

References

Allport, G.W. (1954). *The nature of prejudice.* Reading: Addison-Wesley.

Altman, I. (1993). Challenges and opportunities of a transactional world view: Case study of contemporary Mormon polygamous families. *American Journal of Community Psychology*, 21(2), 135–163. https://doi.org/10.1007/BF00941618

Anderson, J. (2004). Talking whilst walking: A geographical archaeology of knowledge. *Area*, 36(3), 254–261. https://doi.org/10.1111/j.0004-0894.2004.00222.x

Billig, M. (1995). *Banal nationalism.* London: Sage.

Billig, M., Condor, S., Edwards, D., Gane, M., Middleton, D., & Radley, Al. (1988). *Ideological dilemmas: A social psychology of everyday thinking.* London: Sage.

Binnie, J., Edensor, T., Holloway, J., Millington, S., & Young, C. (2007). Mundane mobilities, banal travels. *Social and cultural geography*, 8(2), 165–174. https://doi.org/10.1080/14649360701360048

Bridger, A.J. (2010). Walking as a "radicalized" critical psychological method? A review of academic, artistic and activist contributions to the study of social environments. *Social and Personality Psychology Compass*, 4(2), 131–139. https://doi.org/10.1111/j.1751-9004.2009.00243.x

Bridger, A.J. (2011). Psychogeography and the study of social environments. In P. Reavey (Ed.), *Visual methods in psychology: Using and interpreting images in qualitative research.* Hove: Psychology Press.

Bridger, A.J. (2014). Visualising Manchester: Exploring new ways to study urban environments with reference to situationist theory, the dérive and qualitative research. *Qualitative Research in Psychology*, 11(1), 78–97. https://doi.org/10.1080/14780887.2012.719071

Bridger, A.J. (2015). Psychogeography, anti-psychologies and the question of social change. In T. Richardson (Ed.), *Walking inside out: Contemporary British psychogeography*. London: Rowman and Littlefield.

Bridger, A.J., Emmanouil, S., & Lawthom, R. (2019). The psychogeographical turn in applied social psychology. In K. O'Doherty & D. Hodgetts (Eds.) *The sage handbook of applied social psychology* (pp. 515–529). London: Sage.

Brown, L., & Durrheim, K. (2009). Different kinds of knowing: Generating interview data through mobile interviewing. *Qualitative Inquiry*, 15(5), 911–930. https://doi.org/10.1177%2F1077800409333440

Burnett, J., Cudworth, E., & Tamboukou, M. (2004). Women on dérive: Autobiographical explorations of lived spaces. In *Women and Geography Study Group, Geography and Gender Reconsidered.* CD-ROM, August: 118–141.

Chamberlain, K. (2011). Troubling methodology. *Health Psychology Review*, 5(1), 48–54. https://doi.org/10.1080/17437199.2010.520113

Corral-Verdugo, V., & Pinheiro, J.Q. (2009). Environmental psychology with a Latin American taste. *Journal of Environmental Psychology*, 29(3), 366–374. https://doi.org10.1016/j.jenvp.2008.10.007

Cuba, L., & Hummon, D. M. (1993). A place to call home: Identification with dwelling, community and region. *The Sociological Quarterly*, 34(1), 111–131.

Cushman, E. (1990). Why the self is empty: Toward a historically situated psychology. *American Psychologist*, 45(5), 599–611.

Davis, M., & Monk, D.B. (Eds.). (2008). *Evil paradises: Dreamworlds of neo-liberalism*. New York: The New Press.

Dixon, J., & Durrheim, K. (2000). Displacing place identity: A discursive approach to locating self and other. *British Journal of Social Psychology*, 39(1), 27–44. https://doi.org/10.1348/014466600164318

Durrheim, K., & Dixon, J. (2005). *Racial encounter: The social psychology of contact and desegregation*. London: Taylor & Francis.

Edensor, T. (2008). Walking through ruins. In T. Ingold & L. Vergunst (Eds.) *Ways of walking: Ethnography and practice on foot* (pp. 123–141). Aldershot: Ashgate.

Foucault, M. (1967). *Of other spaces: Utopias and heterotopias*. Architecture/Mouvement/Cotinuité. October 1984: "Des Espace Autres," March 1967. Trans by Jay Miskowiec.

Giddens, A. (1991). *Modernity and self-identity: Self and society in the late modern age*. Stanford: Stanford University Press.

Gifford, R. (2014). Environmental psychology matters. *Annual Review of Psychology*, 65, 541–579. https://doi.org/10.1146/annurev-psych-010213-115048

Gotham, K.F. (2002). Marketing Mardi Gras: Commodification, spectacle and the political economy of tourism in New Orleans. *Urban Studies*, 39(10), 1735–1756. https://doi.org/10.1080%2F00420980220000002939

Harris, P.B., McBride, G., Ross, C., & Curtis, L. (2002). A place to heal: Environmental sources of satisfaction among hospital patients. *Journal of Applied Psychology*, 32(6), 1276–1299.

Hayes, G. (2003). Walking the streets: Psychology and the flâneur. *Annual Review of Critical Psychology*, 1(3), 50–66. https://doi.org/10.1111/j.1559-1816.2002.tb01436.x

Hodgetts, D., Chamberlain, K., & Radley, A. (2007). Considering photographs never taken during a photo-production project. *Qualitative Research in Psychology*, 4(4), 263–280. https://doi.org/10.1080/14780880701583181

Hodgetts, D., Drew, N., Sonn, C., Stolte, O., Nikora, L.W., & Curtis, C. (2010). *Social psychology and everyday life*. Palgrave MacMillan: Basingstoke.

Hodgetts, D., Stolte, O., Chamberlain, K., Radley, A., Groot, S., & Waimarie Nikora, L. (2010). The mobile hermit and the city: Considering links between places, objects and identities in social psychological research on homelessness. *British Journal of Social Psychology*, 49(2), 285–303. https://doi.org/10.1348/014466609X450465

Hook, D. (2007). *Foucault, psychology and the analytics of power*. Basingstoke: Palgrave.

JCB. (2019). JCB Government and Defence – Military Backhoe Loaders. *YouTube*. 22 March 2019. www.youtube.com/watch?v=lqwSMF1UtvI

Keith, M., & Pile, S. (Eds.). (1993). *Place and the politics of identity*. New York: Routledge.

Kusenbach, M. (2003). Street phenomenology: The go-along as ethnographic research tool. *Ethnography*, 4(3), 455–485. https://doi.org/10.1177%2F146613810343007

Lefebvre, H. (1976). *The survival of capitalism*. London: Allison and Busby.

Lefebvre, H. (1991). *The Production of Space*. Oxford: Blackwell Publishing.

Lockley, F. (2019). One of Johnson's biggest billionaire donors profits from Israeli state "war crimes". The Canary. September 7, 2019. www.thecanary.co/uk/analysis/2019/09/07/one-of-johnsons-biggest-billionaire-donors-profits-from-israeli-state-war-crimes/

Lykes, M.B., Blanche, M., & Hamber, B. (2003). Narrating survival and change in Guatemala and South Africa. *American Journal of Community Psychology*, 31(1–2), 79–90. https://doi.org//10.1023/a:1023074620506

Mandipour, A. (2004). Marginal public spaces in European cities. *Journal of Urban Design*, 9(3), 267–286.

Manzo, L.C. (2003). Beyond house and haven: Toward a revisioning of emotional relationships with places. *Journal of Environmental Psychology*, 23(1), 47–61. https://doi.org/10.1016/S0272-4944(02)00074-9

McDonald, M., Bridger, A.J., Wearing, S.L., & Ponting, J. (2017). Consumer spaces as political spaces: A critical review of social, environmental and psychogeographical research. *Social and Personality Psychology Compass*, 11(7). https://doi.org/10.1111/spc3.12325

Merrifield, A. (1993). Place and space: A Lefebvrian reconciliation. *Transactions of the British Institute of Geographers*, 18(4), 516–531.

Miles, S. (2010). *Spaces for consumption*. London: Sage.

Miles, S. (2012). The neoliberal city and the pro-active complicity of the consumer. *Journal of Consumer Culture*, 12(2), 216–230. https://doi.org/10.1177%2F1469540512446881

Military Today. (2021). HMEV Backhoe Loader. *Military Today*. www.militarytoday.com/engineering/hmev.htm

Moser, G., & Uzzell, D. (2003). Environmental psychology. In I.B. Weiner (Series Ed.), Th. Milon & M.J. Lerner (Vol. Ed.), *Handbook of psychology: Vol 5. Personality and social psychology* (pp. 419–445). New York: Wiley.

Nieuwhof, A. (2018). British Firm JCB helps Israel commit war crimes. *The Electronic Intifada*. 29 September 2018. https://electronicintifada.net/blogs/adri-nieuwhof/british-firm-jcb-helps-israel-commit-war-crimes.

Nowell, B.L., Berkowitz, S.L., Deacon, Z., & Foster-Fishman, P. (2006). Revealing the cues with community places: Stories of identity, history and possibility. *American Journal of Community Psychology*, 37(1–2), 29–46. https://doi.org//10.1007/s10464-005-9006-3

On Demand News. (2019). "Get Brexit Done!": Boris Johnson Smashes JCB Tractor Through "Gridlock" Wall. *On Demand News*. 10 December 2019. www.youtube.com/watch?v=4PYU5q1RJv4

Parker, I. (1994). Qualitative research. In P. Banister, E. Burman, M. Taylor, C. Tindall, & I. Parker (Eds.) *Qualitative methods in psychology: A research guide*. Buckingham: Open University Press.

Parker, I. (1996). Postmodernism and its discontents: Therapeutic discourse. *British Journal of Psychotherapy*, 12, 4, 447–460.

Peck, J., & Tickell, A. (2002). Neoliberalising space. *Antipode*, 34(3), 380–404.

Pinder, D. (1996). Subverting cartography: The situationists and maps of the city. *Environment and Planning A*, 28(3), 405–427. https://doi.org/10.1068%2Fa280405

Pink, S. (2004). Performance, self-representation and narrative: Interviewing with video. In C.J. Pole (Ed.), *Seeing is believing? Approaches to visual research studies in qualitative methodology* (Vol. 7, pp. 61–77). Bingley: Emerald. https://doi.org/10.1016/S1042-3192(04)07005-3

Plant, S. (1992). *The most radical gesture: The situationist international in a post-modern age*. London: Routledge.

Radley, A., Chamberlain, K., Hodgetts, D., Stotle, O., & Groot, S. (2010). From means to occasion: Walking in the life of homeless people. *Visual studies*, 25(1), 36–45. https://doi.org/10.1080/14725861003606845

Reggio, G. (1982). *Koyaanisqatski: Life out of balance*. Santa Monica: MGM Entertainment.

Richardson, T. (Ed.). (2015). *Walking inside out: Contemporary British psychogeography*. London: Roman and Littlefield.

Sadler, S. (1998/1999). *The situationist city*. London: MIT Press.

Sheller, J., & Urry, J. (2000). The city and the car. *International Journal of Urban and Regional Research*, 24(4), 737–757. https://doi.org/10.1111/1468-2427.00276

Sheller, M., & Urry, J. (2006). The new mobilities paradigm. *Environment and Planning A*, 38(2), 207–226. https://doi.org/10.1068%2Fa37268

Simmel, G. (1950). The metropolis and mental life. In K.H. Wolff (Ed.), *The sociology of Georg Simmel*. Glen Coe: Free Press.

Sotelo, L.C. (2010). Looking backwards to walk forward. *Performance Research*, 15(4), 59–69. https://doi.org/10.1080/13528165.2010.539880

Spink, M.J.P., & Spink, P.K. (2015). Organizational psychology and social issues. The place of the place. In I. Parker (Ed.), *Handbook of critical psychology*. London: Routledge.

Twigger-Ross, C.L., & Uzzell, D.L. (1996). Place and identity processes. *Journal of Environmental Psychology*, 16(3), 205–220. https://doi.org/10.1006/jevp.1996.0017

Vail, J. (2010). Decommodification and egalitarian political economy. *Politics & Society*, 38(3), 310–346. https://doi.org/10.1177%2F0032329210373069

Voyce, M. (2006). Shopping malls in Australia: The end of public space and the rise of "consumerist citizenship"? *Journal of Sociology*, 42(3), 269–286. https://doi.org/10.1177%2F1440783306066727

Wood, D. (1987). I don't feel that about environmental psychology today. But I want to. *Journal of Environmental Psychology*, 7(4), 417–424. https://doi.org/10.1016/S0272-4944(87)80014-2

Žižek, S. (2011). *Democracy is the enemy*. Retrieved from the London Review of Books website: www.lrb.co.uk/blog/2011/10/28/slavoj-

2

CONCEPTUALISING THE FIELD

In Chapter 1, I defined psychogeography and reviewed key academic literature as well provided a rationale for a psychogeographical approach. In this chapter, I review precursors to psychogeography, founding persons and those associated with the new psychogeographical movement. In this chapter, I will consider contributions to psychogeography from outside of academia, and there are numerous turns into and out of academic work that are necessary to formulate my approach. There are many excellent books on the history and philosophy of walking (Coverley, 2006/2018; Solnit, 2005), and it is not an aim in this book to reproduce yet another historical account of the situationists and their approach to psychogeography. What I want to do in this chapter is to begin conceptualising how the theoretical apparatus of psychogeography and of situationism can then begin to be formulated as a methodology and practice for those who wish to use it in developing their own critical psychological research.

Precursors to psychogeography

A philosophy of walking may arguably begin with Aristotle (c 334–322) and the peripatetic method (known in Greek as 'peripatētikós') whereby he would teach his students about all manner of the state, science and philosophy by walking with them around the walkways of the city. Here, the practice of walking can be considered as a useful teaching method in that it would engage all the students' senses in

DOI: 10.4324/9781315648095-2

thinking, walking, seeing, smelling and hearing. However, the purpose of such walks would not be to directly critique urbanism in order to consider an alternative order of things beyond capitalism. Instead, the aims were much broader in terms of inculcating students in required knowledge to make them into the next generation of workers, i.e. judges and landlords. Hence, the aims were largely to contribute to existing systems and structures rather than to radically change society for the better.

From the time of Ancient Greece to the present day, it is possible to see how certain people began to use walking as a way to understand social conditions and human relationships. Such work has been documented by many poets, artists and political writers such as De Quincey (1821/1886), Baudelaire (2010), Benjamin (1982/2002) and Engels (1845). We move at this point from Ancient Greece to Victorian times and to the emergence of the industrial revolution and the emergence of capitalism. At this point in history, we start to see the first documented accounts of walking as an approach to study the capitalist formation of towns and cities. De Quincey (1821/1886) is regarded as one of the first people who practiced anything resembling a psychogeographical approach. He wandered aimlessly around cities such as Paris and London in an opium haze with no fixed destination in mind and documented such walks in his book titled *Confessions of an English Opium Eater* (1821/1886). The intention of these walks was not to overtly critique the social order of things though some of the ideas raised were quite critical in depicting poverty in London and it does document well the challenging social and material conditions of living in England in the 1800s.

In a different spirit, one could also refer to the poetry and literature of Baudelaire (2010), which arguably is an early example of the idea of the white, male and middle to upper class man, wandering around towns and cities, studying the milieu of everyday life. The figure of the white middle class man has been presented through the theoretical concept of the flaneur, and particular criticisms have been made in recent years by scholars in terms of how such an approach focuses only on mens' experiences of places (Elkin, 2016). Criticisms by academics such as Elkin are rightly made, and later in this chapter and Chapter 3, I discuss the notion of the female walker as flâneuse and feminist psychogeography. The poets, Coleridge and Wordsworth, are also worthy of note as their focus has been on documenting their experiences of the countryside and rural landscapes rather than with any overt criticisms of social systems. Wordsworth (1802/1807) is famously quoted in talking about his experiences of walking around the Lake District, 'I wandered lonely as a cloud'.

It is necessary now to turn to the works of Engels and Benjamin. This work is more overtly political. Engels worked with Marx on formulating a Marxist approach to studying present and future social conditions, and their work combined insights from economics, political theory, science and geography. The key text that I want to focus on here is a book by Engels (1845) titled *The Conditions of the Working Class in England*. In that book, he discussed the conditions of poverty experienced by working-class people in major towns and cities such as London and Manchester. He documented the extremities of poverty in order to show how terrible it was, so that something could be done about it by the legislators, the rulers of state and the people. That work was arguably a precursor to other projects such as Mass Observation, Ethnography and the general media documentation of poverty during the Industrial and early Capitalist eras.

Approximately, 50 years later, Benjamin decided to undertake a study to explore the rise of shopping arcades in Paris, which formed the basis for his book titled the *Arcades Project* (1982/2002). He referred to the shopping arcades as 'temples of commodity capital', which in the present order of things still bears resonance, particularly if this is considered in relation to places such as the Trafford Centre in Manchester or the White Rose Centre in Sheffield. Arguably, it is of importance to investigate places that hold such importance to people if they are considered as temples and particularly given that social scientific inquiry should be based on studying everyday life.

Raban (1974/1984, 16) discusses the importance of making sense of what 'cities do to us and how they change our styles of living and thinking and feeling'. This idea is key to considering the broad aims of a psychogeographical approach, but this should be considered not only in relation to cities but also in relation to towns and the countryside, as will be discussed later in this chapter and also in Chapter 3 where I discuss psychogeographical research in urban and rural contexts.

The more 'radical' approaches to studying everyday life emerge in more recent times, and this is the work that I want to focus on in this part of the book as it takes us to a place where it is possible to begin to formulate a more politically engaged mode of theory and practice. Now it is necessary to begin discussing the work of the Letterist International and then the Situationist International.

The Letterist International was a group of bohemian artists, activists and political theorists who produced art, political writing and film during the times of 1952–1957. They were part of a breakaway group from Isodore Isou's Letterists and included Ivain Chtcheglov, Michèle Bernstein, Alexander Trocchi, Guy Debord and Gill Wolman. The Letterist International took some of their visual motifs from the surrealists and worked on a more politicised and anarchic approach to studying contemporary culture. One member of the group, Kabyle, is alleged to have come up with the term *psychogeography*, which was used to express an ambulatory way to explore the emotional forces of urban environments on human behaviour. A key Letterist that should be referred to here is Ivain Chtcheglov or otherwise known as Gilles Ivain (pseudonym). Ivan Chtcheglov (1958) provided written accounts detailing a psychogeographical approach. Chtcheglov explains in that work how the inner-city districts of Paris, which were predominantly working-class areas, were being demolished to make way for opulent and lavish shopping arcades for the rich and wealthy. In a key article by Chtcheglov (1958) *Formulary for a New Urbanism*, he explains how new urban spaces are where 'each person will live in his own personal 'cathedral'. There will be rooms that produce dreams better than drugs, and houses where it will be impossible to do anything but love'. During the short time in which the Letterist International was in operation, they conceptualised many key terms in order to undertake psychogeographical studies of urban areas such as Paris and London. Amongst their key concepts were the dérive and the detournement. These two terms along with the practice of psychogeography will be returned to in the next part of this chapter where I go onto discuss the work of the Situationist International. It is their work that it is now important to focus on in more depth and to explore how it informs the psychogeographical psychology approach formulated in this book.

The situationists and psychogeography

The Situationist International emerged in the mid-to-late 1950s as a reaction against the capitalist gentrification of towns and cities. They were concerned with the encroachment of capitalism into their everyday lives. The situationists included anarchists, Marxists, artists, intellectuals and political activists. Their aims, tactics and strategies were to work towards the downfall of capitalist society. They believed that radical theory and practice could not exist in universities and other such academic contexts as any radical potential of knowledge would eventually be recuperated by those in power and the bourgeois institutions in which such academics worked. The intellectual terrain for the situationists was that of the streets and bars of Paris and London. The situationists were typically presented in historical accounts as being led by Debord and by the men in the group though such accounts omit the important contributions of its female members such as Michèle Bernstein and Alice Becker-Ho and the generation of political theory and situationist novels, notably, *All the King's Horses* (2004/2008), *The Night* (1961/2013) and *After the Night* (2013). Despite the important contributions that situationist theory makes to a critique of capitalism, it was unfortunate that many patriarchal assumptions informed the values and constitution of the group. Often, the female members of the group would cook and clean whilst its male members could do the 'important' work of writing situationist texts. One member of the situationists explained that:

> One of the curious things about the IS [sic] was that it was extraordinarily anti-feminist in its practice. Women were there to type, cook supper and so on. I rather disapproved of this. Michèle has been an extraordinarily powerful and perceptive mind which is shown by the fact that she is among the most important literary critics in France today. A lot of the theory, particularly the political theory, I think originated with Michèle rather than Debord, he just took it over and put his name to it.
>
> *(Rumney, 2010, n.p.)*

The issue that Rumney therefore shows a serious limitation in situationist theory and practice and something that will be addressed in how I attempt to configure a feminist pschogeographical approach. This will be discussed in more detail in Chapter 3 where I discuss a feminist psychogeographical approach alongside vignettes of research.

Guy Debord (1958, n.p.) was the leading member of the Situationist International, and he provided one of several key definitions of psychogeography as 'the study of the precise laws and specific effects of the geographic environment, consciously organised or not, on the emotions and behaviours of individuals'. Those readers familiar here with the literature of environmental psychology and social psychological research on place may consider that Debord's quote looks remarkably similar to definitions provided in environmental and social psychology textbooks and they would not be wrong. Though if one interrogates the definition provided here by Debord, there are important theoretical distinctions that need to be considered in relation to situationist and psychological accounts. There is arguably some attempt made by Debord in the quote above to present situationist psychogeography as a science in terms of the establishment of laws and effects in relation to studying behaviour and environments. However, there is also an underpinning psychoanalytic argument with the use of the wording 'consciously organised or not' with the 'not' possibly referring to unconscious processes. As readers in psychology will know, psychoanalysis and cognitive science are not good 'bed fellows' even though psychoanalysis runs deep into the historical origins of psychology (Burman, 1994). Secondly, the aims of the situationist approach to studying environments is one with a politically engaged purpose, which can be contrasted to mainstream environmental and social psychological criteria of neutrality, detached observer standpoint and cognitive science. Moreover, the placing of environments in situationist work is quite different from that in cognitive psychology. Community critical psychologists such as Darrin Hodgetts et al. (2010, 287) have argued that environments should not be viewed simply as 'backdrops to social processes'. In this work, it is argued that psychological research should be political research. It is arguable also that many of the arguments provided by Western European and U.S. American psychologists serve to legitimise the principles of individualism and personal human experience (Corral-Verdugo and Pinheiro, 2009). Other cultural geographers such as Ingold (1993, 152) have stated that what is needed in the social sciences is for a study of peoples' 'lived everyday involvement in the world' and how peoples' experiences are actually suffused via dominant and alternative societal discourses. The study of peoples' experiences of everyday life is something that was considered in a political manner by one of the leading situationists, Raoul Vaneigem (1967), in his most well-known work, *The Revolution of Everyday Life*. He argued that social life is bound up with capitalist social relations where people are alienated from themselves and others. Vaneigem argued that it is important to reclaim back our lives from capitalism in order to lead to greater freedoms, which would be beyond a capitalist order of things. The point of the activities of the Situationist International was therefore 'to create situations' that would lead to radical social change and to a world beyond capitalism. They did not envision that they would make the changes themselves though they did believe that through their work this would sow the seeds for revolt to occur and this would be actualised by the people. The situationists entered into conflict with Henri Lefebvre (1983), and as he stated in his own words:

> They [the SI] more of less said to me … 'what you call "moments" we call "situations", but we're taking it further than you. You accept as "moments" everything that has occurred in the course of history: love, poetry, thought. We want to create new moments'.

Lefebvre wanted to study the richness of experience. However, the Situationist International sought to create new types of experience. Lefebvre simply wanted to reinterpret life, whereas the situationists wanted radical social change. As Debord himself argued, 'the transformation of the world is not only a realisation of philosophy but also a realisation of art'. Bunyard argues on the situationist strategy that:

> It was not enough, in other words, to demonstrate the inadequacies of the present: new forms of cultural activity and behaviour were required in order to move beyond the failings of a decomposing society'.
>
> *(Bunyard, 2018, 133)*

The situationists critiqued the social conditions of 'the present' with many techniques including walking as a critical observational method, theoretical writing and the production of novels, films and political pamphlets. Their aims were to reappropriate existing cultural objects and to use this for the purpose of anti-capitalist communications. Indeed, the situationists 'conducted walks in towns and cities to challenge the capitalist ordering of space and to begin to imagine what environments could look like if these contexts were not underpinned by the concerns of capitalism and consumerism' (Bridger, 2014, 80). The time in which the situationists developed their key theories and practices was amidst the capitalist gentrification of towns and cities such as Paris, Amsterdam and London. Many of the situationists were based in the inner-city districts of Paris, and they witnessed the rampant changing form of their everyday places and spaces with whole areas of working-class houses being demolished and areas being rebuilt to make way for lavish and spectacular shopping areas for those

Parisians who were ostensibly rich and wealthy. One way in which the situationists depicted the demolition of the poor working-class areas of Paris was through a detourned map, known as the Naked City map (Debord and Jorn, 1957). Understandably, situationists such as Chtcheglov (1958) were dismayed at such rapid capitalist social change in Paris. Therefore, during the late 1950s to the mid-1960s, the situationists conceptualised the idea of psychogeography as a way to critique the changing form of towns and cities via a critical anti-capitalist mode of analysis. Sadler, a critical historian, writing about the situationists explained that psychogeography could be theorised as a type of 'therapy' and as a means of 'exciting the senses and the body' in order to 'rescue drifters from the clutches of functionalism' (Sadler, 1999, 80). The situationists' analysis of cities and towns was not merely to make sense of such 'everyday' places and spaces but also to provide a critique of urbanism. They wanted to make 'new situationist ambiences', which would lead to inevitable 'permanent change' (Khatib, 1958).

The situationists developed particular techniques in order to critique the consumer capitalist ordering of things. Their two main concepts were détournement and the dérive. Détournement involved a sabotaging and reappropriation of existing signs whether they be word, image or place. The process of detourning signs could often include altering mass media signs such as newspaper articles, political speeches and advertising billboards. The radical art collective Neue Slowenische Kunst N.S.K. is one example where they use the situationist tactic of detournement. In their past work, they have appropriated the language and imagery of fascism and totalitarianism and have done things such as creating a state that operates without borders and where they can issue their own passports to those who agree with the principles of their group (https://passport.nsk.si/en/about_us). The second concept, the dérive, can best be understood in relation to the practice of psychogeographical walking. The concept of the dérive refers to random walking, and Debord (1958, n.p) explains that:

> Dérives involve playful-constructive behaviour and awareness of psychogeographical effects, and are thus quite different from the classic notions of journey or stroll. In a dérive one or more persons during a certain period drop their relations, their work and leisure activities, and all their other usual motives for movement and action, and let themselves be drawn by

> the attractions of the terrain and the encounters they find there. Chance is a less important factor in this activity than one might think: from a dérive point of view, cities have psychogeographical contours, with constant currents, fixed points and vortexes that strongly encourage and discourage entry into or exit from certain zones.

Thus, doing dérives was a way to explore places and spaces and to enable an opening up of the senses and the mind consciously and unconsciously. Such walks were meant to have a dream-like aspect to them (Wollen, 2001) and were meant to disorientate people spatially and mentally. The psychoanalytic concept of free association is useful to consider here in relation to doing dérives, and it is useful to consider Freud's account of a train journey as a way to demonstrate the concept of free association and how that psychoanalytic concept is akin to psychogeographical investigations, 'Act as though, for instance, you were a traveller sitting next to the window of a railway carriage and describing to someone outside the carriage the changing views of which you see outside' (Freud, 1913, 135). The 'unplanned and unstructured' aspect to dérives was meant to produce new insights, observations and chance encounters with others (Jenks and Neves, 2007, 7). Wollen (2001, 3) argued that, 'Debord's basic idea is that this project of wandering through the city should be determined not by any preconceived plan, but by the attractions or discouraging counter-attractions of the city itself'. Importance is attached to the practice of the dérive and to working out the key pushes and pulls of the various spaces and places and to consider what we are drawn towards and what we are repelled from. In this context, there is something of the language of scientific investigation and of physics and atoms. Dérives are therefore practices of walking to consider how spaces and places can be appropriated and changed for alternative uses. Such walks can be used to take people out of the routine ways in which they would move through everyday spaces and places in order to get to work, for leisure and other purposes (Debord, 1958; Kotányi and Vaneigem, 1961). Such walks were not simply aimless but were meant to lead to new imaginings and understandings of everyday spaces and places and to consider how things could be beyond a capitalist order of things. However, with the rise of the internet and digital communications, this can also include navigating the internet and going from one place to another such as Google, Facebook and email.

It could be argued that the situationists managed to appropriate the notion of scientific experimentation with the conceptualisation of psychogeography and key concepts such as the dérive and detournement. Their approach to studying capitalist gentrification was quite playful and in a sense was experimental in terms of a play with signifiers and what things could mean. The situationists wanted to disrupt the dominant connections of capitalist signifiers to objects and replace those capitalist signifiers with anti-capitalist signifiers. Here it is useful to consider the work of De Saussure (1974) and Barthes (1972) and their work on semiology and signifiers as this provides an important framework through which to disrupt the mythological framework of the ruling classes (Barthes, 1972). What their work contributes is to a consideration of signifiers of capitalism and consumerism in major towns and cities in Europe and the United States. The central aims of psychogeographical investigations were therefore to question the dominant ways that we see, experience and interact with environments and to do this to critique and challenge naturalised associations between capitalism and the objects. The concerns of the situationists and writers such as De Saussure and Barthes are still arguably of importance as we live in times in which consumer capitalism reigns supreme in Europe and the Western world. Stephen Miles (2010, 8), a cultural geographer, explains that consumerism has become a 'thoroughly cultural phenomenon that serves to legitimise capitalism on an everyday basis'. It would appear then that the work of the situationists still holds relevance to understanding the contemporary order of things in society as well as psychology. However, some academics would argue that the work of the situationists holds little value in today's context and that their work needs to be wholly revised and updated to understand the order of things today. Those arguments seem of relevance, but it is important not to lose key situationist concepts such as detournement, the derive and psychogeography. In the next part of this chapter, I turn to the work of academics, writers, artists and activists involved with post situationism and the new psychogeographical movement.

Post situationism and the new psychogeographical movement

In this part of the chapter, I am going to discuss the work of key thinkers involved in post situationism and what has been referred to as the new psychogeography movement (Richardson, 2015; Smith, 2015). By referring to the term *post situationists*, I refer to literary writing that has been informed by the situationists but where the authors might not directly acknowledge themselves as situationists. The situationists were quite averse to calling themselves situationists and explained that where anyone did they would obviously be anti-situationists (Black, n.d). I start here with key authors and film makers including Will Self, Patrick Keiller, W.G. Sebald, Iain Sinclair and J.G. Ballard. Whilst these writers are neither psychologists nor critical psychologists, they have contributed important accounts of what it is like to live in contemporary urban and rural living conditions and what some of the problems are with the consumer capitalist order of things and the focus on television as spectacle and car culture. Their work is often fictional, biographical and historical and is key to providing literary accounts of the current urban times, particularly within Western Europe and the United States.

Then there are key post situationist groups that are important to discuss briefly, and these include Manchester Area Psychogeographic (MAP) www.twentythree.plus.com/MAP/index.html and the London Psychogeographical Association (LPA) https://en.wikipedia.org/wiki/London_Psychogeographical_Association. These two groups were informed in varying degrees by the theories of the Situationist International with MAP often being positioned as more focused on the occult and with the LPA as being more focused on the classic political standpoint of situationism. In reality though, there was much convergence between the two groups. The next couple of groups include the Bureau of Public Secrets, directed by Ken Knabb (2007) who also authored, edited and translated the writings of the Situationist International. The San Francisco Bay area situationists are another important group, and there was also another group known as Boal et al. (2005).

These groups along with the writings of authors such as Self, Sinclair and Keiller informed the sort of approach that I formulate as my psychogeographical approach, though I was and am still keen to focus more on a political analysis and application of situationist theory and practice as opposed to focusing on the occult and the study of phenomena such as ley lines. At this phase in my work I, was ready to apply the concepts of situationist theory to study where I was currently living, and in order to do that, I decided to design and conduct a dérive at the Manchester Arndale Centre in the United

Kingdom during the Buy Nothing Day event of 2004. I was distributing situationist pamphlets outside Selfridges in Manchester city centre, and on a Buy Nothing Day stall, I started talking with Morag Rose. We later formed a working friendship and organised various psychogeographical walks across Manchester including the Lunar Water Walk and, in collaboration with Bob Dickinson from MAP, organised the levitation of Beetham's Tower. Many of these walks centred around the gentrification of the Northern Quarter in Manchester, though we would often wander around other parts of the city such as around Deansgate and into Salford Quays. As with any situationist walks, they would invariably conclude in local pubs where this gave us an opportunity to discuss where we had wandered to and where we would share photos and decide on future walks. In subsequent years, these meetings garnered many more people, and Morag, Phaedra and Prenna decided to name the group the Loiterers Resistance Movement. At the time, I wasn't so sure about the name of the group as I was concerned with institutionalising what we did as a 'thing'. Coinciding with the emerging interest with the group, various academics and activists and I organised a psychogeographical conference in Manchester as we wanted to bring together those involved with engaging in situationist, post situationist and psychogegraphical research and practice. With financial support from the Psychology Department at Manchester Metropolitan University, we were able to organise an international psychogeographical conference and festival, and we called this *Territories Reimagined: International Perspectives https://trip2008.wordpress.com*. The TRIP conference organising committee included Geoff Bunn (MMU), Mark Rainey (curator at Urbis), Bob Dickinson (BBC Radio journalist and co-director of MAP), Morag Rose (LRM), Julian Holloway (MMU), John Binney (MMU) and Anna Powell (MMU). The conference side of the programme included a range of academic talks, walks and performances, which took place within the University. However, we were wary to not want to exclude those who wanted to contribute but who would not feel comfortable or would not wish to be in an academic context. We decided to create a fringe programme, which was called the *Get Lost Festival* and which was curated by Morag Rose http://nowhere-fest.blogspot.com/2008/. As part of the *Get Lost Festival*, which ran alongside the TRIP programme, we hosted exhibitions and other events at venues such as the Green Room, the Zion Centre and Urbis in Manchester. Despite the challenges involved in organising and running such a large-scale event across multiple locations across the city, many delegates and those attending appeared to enjoy the proceedings. Ten years on and the conference and festival have not re-emerged again, though many of the organising committee have been involved in organising other psychogeographical talks, conferences, festivals and exhibitions, including:

- Rose's curated exhibition at the Peoples' History Museum in Manchester, Loitering with Intent: The Art and Politics of Walking and first Sunday of each month psychogeographical walks in Manchester, with the Loiterers Resistance Movement http://thelrm.org
- Bridger and colleagues with the annual 4th World Congress of Psychogeography at the University of Huddersfield and other venues across Yorkshire https://4wcop.org

Two key figures associated with the naming of the 'new psychogeographical movement' include Smith and Richardson. Smith's work arises largely from the area of theatre, literature and performance studies. Smith (2015) has argued previously to move beyond situationist theory and practice and explains that sci-fi, fiction and performative practice can envision and effect real social change. However, it seems mistaken to assume that the situationists did not change anything through their endeavours, and indeed, the situationists argued that they sowed the seeds of revolt that actualised the riots of May 1968. It is also arguable that the work of the situationist, Alexander Trocchi (1964), with the Sigma Files prefigured the internet. I return to the question of situationism and social change later in this chapter where I discuss the contributions of the post situationist group Class Wargames, led by Barbrook and Tompsett. What I see as the limits of previous academic research on situationist theory and practice is the lack of a development of a methodology and theoretical framework. Later in this chapter, I set out the key concepts and assumptions underpinning a psychogeographical psychological approach. But first it is necessary to review a further contribution by schizocartographer and post situationist Richardson (2015) in her edited collection of essays on UK psychogeography titled *Walking Inside Out: Contemporary British Psychogeography*. This book exists as the most relevant and up-to-date account of the diversity of psychogeographical research across the United Kingdom and includes contributions in areas including legal psychogeography (Bennett, 2015), cultural theory (Richardson, 2015), geography (Henshaw, 2015) and psychology (Bridger, 2015). Other psychogeography books whilst useful, interesting and well written focus on more 'London-centric' accounts of the movement (Coverley, 2006/2018), though the more recent update of the book includes Manchester, Leeds and Exeter flavours of psychogeography (Coverley, 2006/2018).

In the current context of the 2020s, much of the main psychogeographical work emerges in areas including art and performance studies (i.e. Walking Artists Network, Heddon, Samuels, Wrights and Sites, Smith and mythogeography, 2015), human geography (Rose, 2015) and feminist writers and groups (Elkin, 2016). What I want to do in the next part of this chapter is to move the debates on situationism and psychogeography into the later phase of Debord's work with the Situationist International where he discussed the metaphor of wargaming and political theory. This then makes it necessary to connect up with arguments by academics and artists including Parker (2007), Barbook (2014) and the Neue Slowenische Kunst (www.nskstate.com. Therefore, in the next part of this chapter, it is important to consider the situationist notion of 'play' in relation to a very different consideration of spatial relations of power and movement and to the social conditions of consumer capitalism and neoliberalism.

Psychogeography and wargaming

As argued previously, psychogeography and situationist theory should not be merely about radical walking or about considering psychogeography just as a qualitative method such as the interview and other observational methods. Instead, psychogeography and situationist theory should be considered as a way of thinking about the world, as an epistemological approach and philosophy. It should also be considered as an 'artillery' of various tactics, methods and strategies, in order to work towards creating change in the social world. Broadening out the scope of methods to also refer to tactics and strategy also means that such an approach can be considered not just as a neutral and objective research method but also as a form of political practice.

Arguably, too much focus has been taken by scholars, artists and activists in relation to the situationists' work on psychogeography from the late 1950s to the late 1960s. In the situationists' later work beyond the 1960s, Debord writes about psychogeographical theory and practice in relation to a politics of wargaming and he explains why such an approach is a more useful way to critique the capitalist order of things. Such work is central to the sort of approach advocated in this book. In Debord's *Panegyric* (1989), he writes that:

> I have studied the logic of war. Moreover, I have succeeded, a long time ago, in presenting the basics of movements as a board game: the forces of contention and the contradictory necessities imposed on the operations of each of the two parties. I have played The Game of War and, in the often difficult conduct of my life, I have utilised lessons from it … On the question of whether I have made good use of such lessons, I will leave to others to decide.

In the discipline of psychology, the standard set of methods includes laboratory studies, experiments, interviews, observational methods and analysis of pre-existing data (i.e. political speeches, news reports and advertisements). However, to consider the idea of a board game as a method and as an object of serious study seems anathema to the usual modes of psychological research. However, if we take apart how the word 'experiment' comes to bear meaning, it could be linked to the notion of play and a play with meaning and to critically consider what comes to be produced as knowledge. In this work, one of the central arguments is to study relations of power as spatial relations. So therefore, if it is possible to transpose social life into a board, we can then potentially map social relations. Debord (1989) talks of the 'forces of contention and the contradictory necessities', and this can link back to his earlier arguments about how certain environments 'encourage or discourage entry' and how certain places may attract or repel us (Debord, 1958). In the quote above, it is possible to infer that such a game has had important personal and political ramifications, both in terms of understanding his place in the world as well as understanding and providing a more detailed critique of the consumer capitalist order of things as they were in the late 1980s.

In 1987, Debord and Becker-Ho published their approach to situationist wargaming with their book titled *A Game of War*. In the preface to the first edition of the book, published in 1987, Debord writes that the game is meant to represent the realities of warfare, with all the difficulties and adversities that army troops would typically encounter. Debord (1989) quotes Marcus Hieronymus Vida's (1527) poem about chess, Scacchia Ludus, which he argues can be applied to the situationist *Game of War*, Ludimus effigiem belli: What we play is a representation of war. Game of war is similar to chess in many respects but is played on a larger board with terrain, more figures and a greater range of movements. He also compares the game to poker but not in relation to the element of chance but to the combative aspects of poker. Debord's game, also known as *Kriegspiel*, sets out two opposing armies of equal footing, who seek through movement and battle to outwit each other. However, the game is not simply about destroying the opponents' army, and indeed, one can win the game by breaking down the opponents' lines of communication and their resources. Each army must stay in direct contact with its lines of communication. Strategy and tactics within the game are governed by Clausewitz's (1997) theories on war and are informed by 18th-century warfare, namely, the French Revolution and the wars that Napoleon Bonaparte fought against Wellington and others. The board on which one plays the game is actually a blank sheet with 500 squares and includes mountain squares, mountain passes, forts and arsenals. The implementation of the mountains means that armies cannot move through the mountains, cannot shoot against the enemy and also cannot move arsenals or create communications between army units. Each army starts at the North or South side of the board and moves one unit per square and two units for cavalry and mounted artillery, with up to five units moving at any one time. The units are composed of infantry, cavalry, foot artillery and mounted artillery. Units can fire in straight lines only, but this can be not only horizontal or vertical but also diagonal. As a game, it can replicate many of the key dialectics of conflict though it does have certain limits of which any simulated game of war would have, i.e. gauging the morale of the troops and how that could impact on battle ability and the effects of night and day on army visibility, movement and fighting ability. There are important conclusions that can be drawn from wargames played by the Class Wargames collective. One key wargame includes Debord's Game of War. The Class Wargames collective includes key figures including Richard Barbrook (Politics Department, University of Westminster) and Fabian Tompsett (LAP, Author and co-editor with Alastair Bonnett for *Transgressions: A Journal of Urban Exploration*). They refer to themselves as 'an avant-garde group of artists, activists and theoreticians engaged in the production of works of ludic subversion in the bureaucractic society of controlled consumption' (www.classwargames.net). In their online manifesto, it includes the following information:

- puts on participatory performances of Guy Debord's *The Game of War* and other subversive politico-military games;
- investigates gaming as a metaphor for social relations under repressive neoliberalism;
- celebrates the craft skills of gamers as artistic expression;
- creates a social space where lefties can meet & play with each other;
- re-enacts the proletarian struggles of the past in ludic form;
- trains the militants of the cybernetic communist revolution to come.
- (www.classwargames.net/?page_id=4375)

Such work can be usefully linked back to the sort of work that we should be doing in psychology in connecting research with political practice, and it is the psychogeographical psychological approach that is turned to next in this chapter. In order to better understand the Game of War and what it could potentially contribute to my psychogeographical approach, I bought resin miniatures from Old Crow Models (www.oldcrowmodels.co.uk), painted the miniatures and then printed out and laminated the board with the help of the University of Huddersfield printing services. With the financial support from the Centre for Applied Psychology Research, we were provided with funds to pay for the Class Wargames collective to travel from London to put on a Game of War event for University staff, the general public as well as local wargamers, the Kirklees Crusaders. The work of the Class Wargames collective has been an inspiration for my own work, as will be discussed in the remaining part of this and subsequent chapters.

Psychogeographical psychology

Methodology is key within psychological research, and it is considered as one of the 'badges' of respectable scientific inquiry to have a solid method with clear underpinning criteria. However, the question of methods in relation to doing psychogeographical research is rather a misnomer. The situationists never theorised psychogeography as a method and neither would they have wished to do so for fear of their work being appropriated and neutralised by what they considered as university systems, which were and continue to be informed by capitalist and bourgeois assumptions. The situationists were not wrong and their arguments should still be taken seriously as can be evidenced by the emergence of the critical psychology approach, which, although in its early days was political and radical, has in more recent times become increasingly neutralised and appropriated by neoliberal systems, structures and managerial processes (Parker, 2020). Such ideas thus raise the question of how to do radical research and whether this needs to take place in psychology or if it is necessary to step outside the discipline. In the rest of this chapter, I formulate a theoretical approach to psychogeographical psychology, but I will reflect in later chapters on why such work also needs to take place outside of psychology and outside of universities. I start here with a quote by Parker on the idea of methods in relation to generating research questions:

> Now it is necessary to find a way to open up new ways of thinking about the domain of the 'psychological' – perhaps by refocusing on such things as 'experience', 'subjectivity' or 'interaction' – so that the methodologies we develop follow from the research question.
>
> *(Parker, 2007, 136)*

In order to think properly about 'the domain of the "psychological"', I will first of all present key research questions that have underpinned many of the psychogeographical projects that I have undertaken in recent years. Examples of these projects will be discussed in Chapter 3, but in this chapter, I will outline the theoretical nuts and bolts of my approach to psychogeography.

Here are key research questions that generally inform the psychogeographical approach that I take in my research. These questions are personal, political and reflective:

- What are my gendered experiences of specific environments? Are these places that I would ordinarily visit? Why/Why not?
- What are the emotional and behavioural effects of familiar and unfamiliar environments?
- How do men and women enter and exit environments?
- Are there any noticeable behavioural or emotional differences when moving between different environments?

- What changes need to occur within environments to facilitate possible social change?

I start here with research questions because the methodology should be conceptualised from key questions underpinning research (Parker, 2007). The questions focus on the study of environments and how particular experiences are produced in such contexts and are informed by Khatib's study (1958) of the Les Halles district in Paris as published in the second issue of the Internationale Situationiste pamphlet. My questions are informed by Khatib's approach to psychogeography because these ideas connect with the sorts of things that I want to ask in my research and they are also a useful way to politically study environments. Moreover, the questions he poses are one of the only accounts of what questions can underpin psychogeographical research and they work as a useful template from which to analyse and critique environments. I return back to Khatib's questions in Chapter 3 where I discuss feminist psychogeography and also a dérive that I conducted around Ground Zero in New York, the United States.

Next are the key concepts that underpin my approach to psychogeography, and these are informed by Barbrook's (2014/2015) approach to situationist theory and class wargaming. His approach to situationist theory and to a study of radical politics is quite close to my ontological position, and for this reason, the way in which he discusses key concepts connects with the sort of approach that I develop in this book. His key concepts are psychogeography, participatory creativity, detournement and provocation. I use these key concepts to underpin my approach to psychogeography.

The first concept is that of psychogeography and this has previously been defined earlier in this chapter. For me, this is not just a concept but also a method and theoretical approach. In essence, psychogeography is a critique of urban and rural environments and is an important part of the class struggle against the ruling classes to realise a new non-capitalist order of things. This is indeed a grand aim for psychological research, and this is where such work needs to operate not just in the discipline but also beyond it. I return back to doing psychogeography outside of psychology in Chapter 4 as this is and should be an important way to combine theory and practice and to have practical relevance beyond neoliberal systems and institutions as they are today.

The second key concept is that of detournement and involves a process of taking existing 'text', subverting it and creating new and alternative counter knowledges. The critical psychological method of Foucauldian discourse analysis is one way in which to deconstruct and question dominant discourses though the situationist technique of detournement takes this process further to create counter subversive meanings in order to lead to a creation of new 'situations'. In the previous part of this chapter, I discussed the situationist aim of creating situations, which was meant to lead to revolutionary social change by the masses. Whilst that may be an underpinning aim of some of the more political discourse analytic work, such work has often stopped short of making claims to create radical social change, and indeed, critical psychology as a discipline in more recent times is becoming increasingly neutralised of radical political application. Therefore, in this chapter, the argument is to move from studying discourses and surveillance to focus on the spectacle and creating situations. One example of the situationist technique of detournement is by way of the rock band Laibach, who have detourned and appropriated the imagery of fascism and used it against fascists.

The third concept to discuss here is that of provocation. This concept is about unsettling how things come to bear meaning and how things could be made sense of. One could therefore argue that meaning is never fixed, and as Lacan has argued, there is always an 'incessant sliding of the signified under the signifier' (Lacan, 1977 [1957], 154). The situationist tactic of provocation and detournment are therefore attempts to allocate new signifieds under the signifiers. Examples of provocation include interventions in social settings such as when the Letterists entered the Notre-Dame Cathedral in Paris and posed as monks delivering a sermon to the public on Easter Sunday in 1950. The sermon included an account of how God had died. Clearly, the congregation was outraged by such a sermon. Another example in more recent times is where Babak Fozooni (2004) was due to present a paper at an international critical psychology conference in Bath on his work on Vygotsky and zones of proximal/proletarian development. However, he was so angry at what he considered to be the apolitical range of talks and seminars that the night before his presentation he decided to rewrite the presentation and the next day delivered a new paper titled 'Fuck Critical Psychology'. His paper outraged some audience members on that day.

The fourth concept is that of participatory creativity, which can be viewed as the opposite of neoliberal individualist activity. The aims here are collectivist in terms of enabling people to work together to be creative and to imagine a new order of things. Vaneigem (1967) discusses this concept in relation to group activity and how it can be a way to facilitate 'the self-realisation of each individual'.

These four concepts then form the basis for the way in which I approach psychogeography as an academic. Invariably, my approach to psychogeography is to 'game-ify' social situations and settings and to spatialise social relations of power.

Moreover, in my practice of psychogeography, I connect with discourse theory and to psychoanalysis, and I do this by way of considering spatial relations as discursive relations and then psychoanalysis in relation to attempting to open myself up to how I associate to various environments with the free association technique. This is why I used the example in Chapter 1 of the JCB and Johnson example to trace a metaphorical route from discourse analysis to psychogeography. In Chapter 3, I will discuss some examples of how I draw together these research questions, the concepts and the approaches of discourse analysis and psychoanalysis.

My approach to psychogeography is not simply an account of a particular walking methodology but also a philosophical approach and a way to detourn various social texts whether they be spatial, textual, embodied, and so on. As I position myself as a critical psychologist, I also take seriously the notion of reflexivity, and I see it as important to reflect on my role in and beyond academia. Being able to read, write and wander is a privilege that not everyone is able to do for whatever reasons whether that may be due to social class, ability, gender, and so on. In Chapter 3, I provide examples of my psychogeographical research and writings, which include accounts of individual and group dérives, situationist inspired theatre and fictional stories.

References

Barbrook, R. (2014/2015). *Class wargames: Ludic subversion against spectacular capitalism*. New York: Minor Compositions.

Barthes, R. (1972). *Mythologies*. London: Vintage.

Baudelaire, C.P. (2010). *The painter of modern life: Charles-Pierre Baudelaire*. London: Penguin.

Benjamin, W. (1982/2002). *The arcades project*. London: Harvard University Press.

Bennett, L. (2015). Incongruous steps towards a legal psychogeography. In T. Richardson (Ed.), *Walking inside out: Contemporary British psychogeography* (pp. 59–72). London: Roman and Littlefield.

Bernstein, M. (2004/2008). *All the king's horses*. London: MIT Press.

Bernstein, M. (2013). *The night*. London: Bookworks. (Original work published 1961)

Bernstein, M. (2013). *After the night: Everyone agrees*. London: Bookworks.

Black, B. (n.d). The realisation and suppression of situationism. *Nothingness.org*. http://library.nothingness.org/articles/SI/en/display/242

Boal, I., Clark, T.J., Matthews, J., & Watts, M. (2005). *Afflicted powers: Capital and spectacle in a new age of war*. London: Verso.

Bridger, A.J. (2014). Visualising Manchester: Exploring new ways to study urban environments with reference to situationist theory, the dérive and qualitative research. *Qualitative Research in Psychology*, 11(1), 78–97. https://doi.org/10.1080/14780887.2012.719071

Bridger, A.J. (2015). Psychogeography, anti-psychologies and the question of social change. In T. Richardson (Ed.), *Walking inside out: Contemporary British psychogeography*. London: Rowman and Littlefield.

Bunyard, T. (2018). Critical theory and cultural studies. In B. Best, W. Bonefield, & C. O'Kane (Eds.) *The sage handbook of Frankfurt school critical theory* (pp. 1348–1364).. London: Sage.

Burman, E. (1994). *Deconstructing developmental psychology*. London: Routledge.

Chtcheglov, I. (1958). *Formulary for a new urbanism*. Retrieved from the Situationist International website: www.cddc.vt.edu/sionline/presitu/ formulary.html

Clausewitz, C.V. (1997). *On war*. Ware: Wordsworth Editions.

Corral-Verdugo, V., & Pinheiro, J.Q. (2009). Environmental psychology with a Latin American taste. *Journal of environmental psychology*, 29(3), 366–374. https://doi.org10.1016/j.jenvp.2008.10.007

Coverley, M. (2006/2018). *Psychogeography*. Harpenden: Pocket Essentials.

Debord, G. (1958). *Theory of the dérive*. Retrieved from the Situationist International website: www.cddc.vt.edu/sionline/si/theory.html

Debord, G. (1989). *Panegyric*. Retrieved from the Debordiana website: http://debordiana.chez.com/debordiana.htm

Debord, G., & Becker-Ho, A. (2006). *A game of war*. London: Atlas Press. (Original work published 1987)

Debord, G., & Jorn, A. (1957). The naked city map. In S. Sadler (1999). *The situationist city*. London: MIT Press.

De Quincey, T. (1886). *Confessions of an English opium eater.* London: George Routledge and Sons. (Original work published 1821). Retrieved from the Gutenberg website: www.gutenberg.org/ebooks/2040

De Saussure, F. (1974). *A course in general linguistics*. London: Fontana.

Elkin, L. (2016). *Flâneuse: Women who walk the city in Paris, New York, Tokyo, Venice and London*. London: Chatto and Windus.

Engels, F. (1845). *The conditions of the working class in England*. Retrieved from the Marx/Engels Archive: www.marxists.org/archive/marx/works/download/pdf/condition-working-class-england.pdf

Fozooni, B. (2004). Fuck critical psychology! *International Conference of Critical Psychology*, University of Bath.

Freud, S. (1913). On Beginning the Treatment. In *The Complete Psychological Works of Sigmund Freud, Volume 12: Case History of Schreber, Papers on Technique and Other Works (1911-1913)*. London:Vintage Publishing.

Henshaw,V. (2015). *Urban smellscapes: Understanding and designing city smell environments*. London: Routledge.

Hodgetts, D., Stolte, O., Chamberlain, K., Radley, A., Groot, S., & Waimarie Nikora, L. (2010). The mobile hermit and the city: Considering links between places, objects and identities in social psychological research on homelessness. *British Journal of Social Psychology*, 49(2), 285–303. https://doi.org/10.1348/014466609X450465

Ingold, T. (1993). The temporality of the landscape. *World Archaeology*, 25(2), 152–174.

Jenks, C., & Neves, T. (2000). A walk on the wild side: Urban ethnography meets the flâneur. *Journal for Cultural Research*, 4(1), 1–17. https://doi.org/10.1080/14797580009367183

Khatib, A. (1958). *Attempt at a psychogeographical description of Les Halles*. Retrieved from the Situationist International Website: www.cddc.vt.edu/sionline/si/leshalles.html

Knabb, K. (2007). *Situationist International Anthology*. Ed. Berkley: Bureau of Public Secrets.

Kotanyi, A., & Vaneigem, R. (1961). *Basic programme of the bureau of unitary urbanism*. Retrieved from the Situationist International website: www.cddc.vt.edu/sionline/si/bureau.html

Lacan, J. (1977). The agency of the letter in the unconscious since Freud (A. Sheridan,Trans.). *Écrits:A selection* (pp. 146–178), London: Routledge/Tavistock.

Lefebvre, H. (1983). *Henri Lefebvre on the Situationist International: Interview*. By Kristin Ross, *October 79*, Winter 1997. Retrieved from the Not Bored website: www.notbored.org/lefebvre-interview.html Not Bored on 2nd August 2021.

Miles, S. (2010). *Spaces for consumption*. London: Sage.

Parker, I. (2007). *Revolution in psychology: From alienation to emancipation*. London: Pluto Press.

Parker, I. (2020). *Psychology through critical auto-ethnography: Academic discipline, professional practice and reflexive history*. Abingdon/New York: Routledge.

Raban, J. (1974/1984). *Soft city*. London: Fontana.

Richardson, T. (Ed.). (2015). *Walking inside out: Contemporary British psychogeography*. London: Roman and Littlefield.

Rose, M. (2015). Confessions of an Anarcho-Flâneuse or psychogeography the Mancunian Way. In T. Richardson (Ed.), *Walking inside out: Contemporary British psychogeography* (pp. 147–164). London: Roman and Littlefield.

Rumney, R. (2010). *About the historification of the Situationist International: Ralph Rumney in conversation with Stewart Home*. Retrieved from the Stuart Home website: www.stewarthomesociety.org/interviews/rumney.htm

Sadler, S. (1999). *The situationist city*. London: MIT Press.

Smith, P. (2015). *Walking's new movement*. Dorset: Triarchy Press.

Solnit, R. (2005). *A field guide to getting lost*. London: Penguin.

Trocchi, A. (1964). *Sigma: A tactical blueprint*. Retrieved from the Situationist International website: www.cddc.vt.edu/sionline/si/sigma.html

Vaneigem, R. (1967). *The revolution of everyday life*. Retrieved from the Nothingness website: http://library.nothing-ness.org/articles/SI/en/pub_contents/5

Vida, M.G. (1527). *Scacchia ludus: A poem on the game of chess*. Dublin: S Powell.

Wollen, P. (2001). Situationists and architecture. *New Left Review*, 8(1), 123–139.

Wordsworth, W. (1802/1807). *I wandered lonely as a cloud. Poems, in two volumes*. London: Longman, Hurst, Rees and Orme.

3

DOING PSYCHOGEOGRAPHY

> 'There is no place for psychogeography in a psychology department'.
>
> *(Anon, 2020)*

In this chapter, I provide illustrative examples of my approach to doing psychogeography, and in line with the arguments already presented in this book, I seek to extend such work by moving beyond consideration of psychogeography only as a walking-based practice. I seek to extend the pantheon of what can be done in and outside academic fields of inquiry and why it is important and relevant to consider other modes of theoretical work in the form of fiction and playwriting. Some of the psychogeographical work to date presents merely a series of garden path modes of analysis (Hayes, 2003). What I seek to do in this chapter is to present a range of theoretically based approaches to psychogeography where I consider how I initially used a situationist psychogeographical approach and then how I developed my unique approach as a psychogeographical psychologist and activist. The key theoretical concepts that will be applied to considering psychogeography will include, and as discussed in Chapter 2, psychogeography, participatory creativity, detournement and provocation. Much of the work that I will discuss in this chapter has been informed by my engagement with individuals and groups outside of academia. Academic, artist and activist work have informed the approach that I take to psychogeography. As far as I am aware

DOI: 10.4324/9781315648095-3

at present, I am one of only a few psychologists who is interested in psychogeography and the only one so far that has conceptualised psychogeography as a methodology and how it can contribute to qualitative, feminist and critical psychological research.

This chapter takes a two-part focus in that I will discuss psychogeographical networking in Manchester and then in Huddersfield. Networking is a key word here in terms of how I made connections with people from academic, activist and artistic arenas. Locality is also important in terms of the production of different types of work focusing on urban and rural psychogeographical studies as well as key individuals and groups from respective different contexts.

Henceforth in this chapter, I will begin in talking about how I 'piloted' a psychogeographical study at the site of Arndale Centre in Manchester by drawing on the work of Khatib (1958) and also Debord and Jorn (1957). The Manchester work will be talked about in relation to my readings on Marxism and Situationism, how and why I created a fictional psychogeographical group called the Bored in the City Collective and how I became involved in organising psychogeographical dérives with various people as well as co-organising an international conference and festival, Territories Reimagined International Perspectives (TRIP). The work here then will be discussed in relation to doing a dérive at Ground Zero, New York, with my brother Jack Bridger. The later work formed a key part of my PhD research.

In the next phase of my work that I will discuss in this chapter, where I will account for how I conceptualise psychogeography as a qualitative visual methodology, how I conceptualise psychogeography as a feminist psychological approach and in more recent work where I have developed psychogeography as a group praxis with people with mental health needs and people identifying as allies of the LGBTQ+ (lesbian, gay, bisexual, transgender, queer) movement. My academic work has coexisted alongside my work outside of academia, which has included attending and organising dérives and talks in Huddersfield and other towns, cities and villages for the Leeds Psychogeographical Group, the Huddersfield Psychogeographical Network and the 4th World Congress of Psychogeography. I have also been involved in creating fictional characters and groups such as the Bored in the City Collective and the fictional character of David Bollinger. Also to be discussed in this chapter will be the fictional academic war research group Perudi. The work of Bollinger, Brandenberg and Perudi will be discussed in terms of their contributions to the 4th World Congress of Psychogeography – an annual psychogeographical festival and conference that takes place in Huddersfield and with partner organisations in and around the local area.

Psychogeography in Manchester, New York and Huddersfield

In this part of the chapter, I will discuss how I piloted a psychogeographical methodology at the site of Arndale Centre in Manchester drawing on the work of Khatib (1958) and also Debord and Jorn (1957). The Manchester work will be talked about in relation to my readings on Marxism and Situationism, the formation of the Bored in the City Collective (blogs and pamphlets) and how I became involved in attending and organising psychogeographical dérives with various people as well as co-organising the TRIP festival and conference. This work then went onto inform the dérive that I conducted at Ground Zero, New York, with my brother Jack Bridger and which would then later be written into my PhD as well as a chapter for Reavey's (2011) book.

Manchester

Whilst I was a PhD student in the Discourse Unit at Manchester Metropolitan University, I was trying to work out a way to study the physical space at Ground Zero in New York. At that phase in my research, I had already used discourse and situationist methods to analyse word and image representations of September 11th, 2001 and the aftermath. I was keen to develop more of a radical political standpoint within my research so my then PhD supervisor, Professor Ian Parker, suggested that I read Sadie Plant's (1992) *The Most Radical Gesture: The Situationist International in a Postmodern Age*. The book set me on a path into the work of the situationists, and since then, I have continued to develop that lineage of work into what I present in this book as my approach to psychogeography. Whilst I was reading the work of the situationists, I was also at the same time considering how I might write about their political approach to everyday life within the context of my research. The more political end of critical psychological work is indeed on the Left though not quite as much on the Left as the situationists would position themselves. Other writers have considered the situationists as being 'Ultraleft'. During my days as a postgraduate PhD student and whilst I was reading the work of the situationists, I came across several situationist-inspired groups and individuals who used pseudonyms such as Luther Blissett, Retort and the Melancholic Troglodytes. I was intrigued at first as to why people would want to write anonymously as I thought they would want people to know who they were so that they could reference them in other work as is the standard practice in neoliberal academic practice of referencing oneself and others to maintain and further commodity relations of knowledge. I was grappling at the time with the ideas and practices of the situationists and was considering how to draw on such work in my PhD. Situationist writing is highly theoretical and requires intellectual engagement with the arguments presented therein. There is no easy path into understanding situationism, and it does require some prior understanding of Marxism and Anarchist theory. Other situationist work is presented in the format of comic strips, art and critical film. Many academics involved in discussing situationist psychogeography only go so far as viewing it as an art practice or in an a-theoretical manner. Such approaches do not do justice to the vision of the situationists, and it is important to keep in place the focus of their work and in aiming to create situations for a revolution of everyday life. In this chapter, these and other contributions will be discussed and evaluated.

In order to better understand the concepts and ideas of the situationists and how I might write such an approach into my PhD, I decided to try making my own situationist-inspired comic strips, pamphlets and critical writing. There are some critical psychologists who have written under group pseudonyms with the main one being Beryl Curt. The academics involved with Beryl Curt included Chris Eccleston, Kate Glesson, Nick Lee, Wendy and Rex Stainton Rogers, Paul Stenner and Marcia Worrell. The Curt group (1994) published a book titled *Textuality and Tectonics: Troubling Social and Psychological Science*, and some members of the group explain that this was done as 'an attempt to find ways-of-writing-about-ways-of-working' (Stainton Rogers and Stainton Rogers, 1997, 45). Writing under a pseudonym thus enabled the writers to take more reflective distance from their positions as critical psychologists and to consider the type of knowledge that they produce in a more playful and collectivist manner. The Melancholic Troglodytes (2003) is another example in relation to their editing of a special issue of the *Annual Review of Critical Psychology* on anti-capitalisms, as discussed in Chapter 2. Writing under a pseudonym in that journal enabled the authors to write in a way that can be more critical of critical psychology than would be possible through using one's own name. For surely, if one is to be properly critical of one's discipline, then one should step outside of it to consider the value of such knowledge from other approaches and perspectives, namely, in this context the contribution of the critical psychological approach to enabling radical social change. In that special issue, the Melancholic Trogloytes consider critical psychological work as being either revolutionary or counterrevolutionary. One could argue that psychogeography could fit within what could be referred to as postpsychology, and this will be returned to as a key point of discussion in the final chapter of this book.

On the basis of such work as discussed previously here, I had thought about particular pseudonyms that I could write under and decided to draw on a quote from Ivan Chtcheglov's (1958) 'Formulary for a new urbanism', where he talks about the idea that 'we are bored in the city'. I chose that particular quote as I wanted to make a point about the banality of urban environments, how such contexts are entirely focused on consumer capitalism and how such contexts can make citizens feel bored. From the term 'we are bored in the city', I refined this down to a pseudo group name, 'Bored in the City'. I got to work on writing situationist-inspired pamphlets and fanzines, which were eventually distributed at the Basement centre on Lever Street in Manchester, to members of the general public outside Selfridges in Manchester on 'Buy Nothing Day' in 2002 and also via the Bored in the City collective blog.

I found it a very useful way to conceptualise and bring together my understanding of situationist theory and practice by writing under a pseudonym and by writing for an audience that would not necessarily be academic. Writing in that way enabled me to explore different writing styles and ways of making arguments that then informed how I wrote my PhD. However, there was a time during my PhD when my engagement with situationist texts took me so far away from my thesis that I unlearnt what I knew about how to write academically. My PhD viva was a terrible experience, though I learnt a lot from it and made sure that I gained a more solid grounding in the work of Foucault, discourse theory and a critical psychological approach to studying the mass media. Some of the key issues with the thesis were surrounding the assumption of audiences as 'cultural dupes' and how a

Marxist position assumes a monolithic notion of people as oppressors or as being oppressed. Such an assumption connects with key ideas underpinning situationist theory and does not fit with a Foucauldian approach to discourse analysis or with critical psychology as a grand overarching approach. There are then clear challenges and dangers in relation to taking political positions in research and how such stances line up with positions in psychology such as Foucauldian discourse analysis, critical psychology and with what can and cannot be assumed about people and how they make sense of and experience the world.

With my writing under the pseudonym of the Bored in the City and then with the successful completion of PhD on developing psychogeography as a qualitative methodology, I was then confident in being able to do psychogeographical work as well as how to write about it in academic psychological arenas. I have chosen to write psychogeography into various areas of psychology including social psychology, visual methods, qualitative research methods, feminist psychology and community psychology.

The first psychogeographical work that I conducted included a series of autoethnographic dérives around the Manchester Arndale Centre in the United Kingdom. That work was carried out as a way to conceptualise how to do dérives with a view to doing a site-specific investigation at the site of the World Trade Centre attacks in New York, the United States. I attempted to use a situationist psychogeographical approach as close to how I thought that the situationists would have used the approach in order to assess the benefits and limits of it and to consider how I might use such an approach in my own work. I needed to see how their ideas and theories worked in practice by replicating the situationist dérive. This didn't mean that I was trying to be a 'traditional' situationist but rather that I was doing as what would usually be done in psychological research in terms of testing pre-existing methods and then considering the usefulness of such methods in one's own work. I had come under 'fire' in one international conference presentation where I was accused of being 'too situationist' and not having done enough in terms of contributing to new psychogeographical research.

In the early stages of my psychogeographical research whilst I was a PhD student, I focused on drawing on Khatib's (1958) account of doing dérives at the Les Halles district in Paris. What I tried to do with this initial psychogeographical work was to understand how to 'do' situationist psychogeography and what such an approach might look like in my work as a critical psychologist. Given my position as a critical psychologist, my focus on the use of the approach was methodological and theoretical, and I also wanted to consider how such an approach could be used to critique the capitalist order of things. Given the context of Manchester at the time, it was also during the time of introducing antisocial behaviour orders and installing closed circuit surveillance cameras around the city. Therefore, my use of psychogeography also included some critique of themes including surveillance and privacy as well as consumer capitalism. Most importantly though, my use of doing psychogeography in Manchester and around specifically the Arndale Centre was to work out how to do a dérive at Ground Zero in New York. Like Ground Zero in New York, the Arndale Centre in Manchester had also been subject to a terrorist attack, and this made it a useful context in which to explore the usefulness of a psychogeographical approach to study such contexts. In one of Debord's key papers (1955, 1958), he explains that one can either do site specific investigations of place or do random explorations of environments. With the Arndale Centre dérive, I chose to do a site-specific investigation (Bridger, 2014) and I conducted this study on my own as opposed to other projects, which will be discussed later in this chapter.

New York

My PhD research at Ground Zero in New York City was worked into a book chapter (Bridger, 2011) in Reavey's edited collection of papers by critical, community and qualitative psychologists (Reavey, 2011). In 2020, a new and revised version of the book was published (Reavey, 2020), which includes further contributions from psychology academics across the globe. Why I discuss my contribution to this book project here is due to the importance of developing visual methodological approaches in psychology and how this 'maps' onto the development of a psychogeographical approach in psychology. At the time that the first book was published, the use of visual methods in psychology was in its 'infancy' with only scant research and publications, such as Parker et al.'s (1999) *Critical Textwork* and Rose's (2003) *Visual Methodologies: An Introduction to Researching with Visual Methods*. Indeed, and as Willig (2011) points out in the foreword to Reavey's (2020) book, there is a 'creative potential of visual approaches and it helps to remove the study of everyday experience from what

Reavey so appropriately describes as 'the grip of language-based methodologies' (Chapter 1, 3). My psychogeographical research at Ground Zero formed the second formal based project that I have undertaken, and it is discussed here in terms of how it was drawn on in order to develop and extend visual methodological approaches in psychology and to argue for a turn to place and a spatial turn in psychology. In that work, I demonstrated an analysis focusing on maps and urban cities to study places in relation to discourses of emotions, drawing on psychogeography, critical psychology and urban theory. The justification for a place-based method of analysis was drawn from the works of (Barnes and Duncan 1992, 5) 'paintings, maps and landscapes' as well as narrative psychologists (Burnett et al., 2004), lesbian feminist critical psychologists (Grup de Lesbianes Feministes, 2004; Precarias a la Deriva, 2004), urban theorists and Marxists (Harley, 1988a, 1988b, 1992; Thrift, 2004) and critical psychologists (Rose, 1999).

To do that, I referred to psychogeography as a walking-based methodology, as a narrative form of documenting psychogeographical walks and in terms of the process of created subverted and creative 'artistic' maps. To illustrate the research, I focused the study on Ground Zero in New York City, and this formed the final phase of analysis in my PhD, which was focused on critically interpreting the events of September 11th, 2001 and the aftermath. The previous analytical chapters of my PhD focused on analysing word and image representations of September 11th and the aftermath using discourse, semiology and situationist analyses of newspaper reports and video footage from UK newspapers and television sources. After having conducted discursive, semiological and situationist analysis on words and images relating to September 11th, 2001, I was curious to consider how to go about analysing the physical space of Ground Zero. As mentioned previously in this book, my then PhD supervisor, Ian Parker, suggested reading the work of the situationists and their approach to psychogeography, and this provided a suitable political and practical way in which to study Ground Zero, thus extending the previous analytical work, that I had already undertaken in the thesis.

Before visiting the site of Ground Zero, I consulted some maps of Downtown Manhatten and checked where the World Trade Centre had previously been located. I decided to walk a route around the World Trade Centre and to draw on Debord's (1958) notion of a "site-specific" dérive. I would use a notepad to document reflections and would take photographs during the walk. I had anticipated at the time that I would document the dérive as a reflective narrative account akin to the type produced by colleagues such as Burnett et al. (2004). This account would be further informed by critical psychology, cultural theory and feminist reflections. The process of the walk would be detourned and made into a dérive because we would be using a map of Bangkok to navigate ourselves around Ground Zero.

In that work, I drew on two key concepts, which were detournement and the dérive. Detournement refers to an attempt to change and to divert from what things come to mean. The concept of the dérive refers to a 'playful' mode of walking in order to critically consider our surroundings with a view to considering what things could look like beyond a capitalist order of things. Later in this chapter, I return to these concepts as I explain how I went on to use those ideas in further work. In my research at Ground Zero, I drew on visual strategies such as photography, autoethnography and making a detourned map of Ground Zero to explore themes that were produced through the research including injury, memory and power relations. It is usually the case that dérives take place in groups of more than several people, though with this particular study it took place with my brother and I. This fitted with what Debord had written in terms of the most productive dérives involving at least two or more people so that they can cross-check their 'findings'. This in a sense appears somewhat akin to the quantitative experimental criterion of reliability and validity. However, whilst the situationists wrote polemical and useful analyses of the impacts of capitalist environments on its citizens, they rarely considered their own political and subjective responses to places and spaces. Whilst there are problems with self-indulgent reflection, I endeavoured in this study to consider personal response in a discursively situated context. Autoethnographic research has indeed been criticised in terms of being too individualistic (Sparkes, 2000) and self-indulgent (Atkinson, 1997). I addressed these issues by considering by personal response as being situated socially, culturally and politically (Holt, 2003).

Therefore, I drew on an autoethnographic approach to the particular study in question. I took inspiration from the work of Burnett et al. (2004) in how they documented their account of a group dérive in London whilst at the same time managing their commitments to work and their families. It should also be noted the trend in qualitative psychology to not consider the political dimensions to research though quite the opposite approach is advocated here.

Clearly there were ethical and emotionally sensitive dimensions to conducting a walk around Ground Zero, given that this was, at the time, several years after the terrible events of September 11th, 2001. We would plan to conduct the dérive three and a half years after those events and needed to ensure that our activities would be done appropriately and with due sensitivity and ethical regard.

My brother and I arrived at Ground Zero ready to conduct the Debordist site-specific study. We were notably jetlagged and tired from having flown via plane from the United Kingdom to the United States, and we were also adjusting to the time zone difference. This added to the sort of disorientation that is conducive to doing situationist dérives. Our initial observations were of speechlessness, shock and horror. Words could not really articulate what it felt like to be at that site. We stood motionless. There were other people also standing in silence, watching over the grey and blank expanse of land that once was the site of the World Trade Centre, once, one of the tallest buildings in New York City. The site of Ground Zero felt like it had been mortally wounded, and we wanted to reflect on what this 'injury' might mean to us. It made me think of a quote by Judith Butler (2004, xii), where she writes that:

> To be injured means that one has the chance to reflect upon injury, to find out the mechanisms of its distribution, to find out who else suffers from permeable borders, unexpected violence, dispossession, and fear, and in what ways.

Therefore, the start of the dérive was in essence not a dérive at all but a memorial. It felt important to honour those who had lost their lives on that day and to pay one's respects. About ten minutes later, we decided to begin the dérive, and we encountered a poster board that detailed information about the design plans for what should go in place of the World Trade Centre, such as parks, memorials, monuments and office buildings. It became quite difficult to randomly walk around the site because Ground Zero had been cordoned off, and so we could only wander in a rectangular route around it. Some areas of Ground Zero were walled off, whereas other areas could only be accessed by going inside publicly accessible buildings such as the World Financial Centre foyer and viewing the site through windows. Once we had walked a quarter way around the site, we decided to use the map of Bangkok to navigate around Ground Zero. But rather than features such as Thai rivers being in view, we had to refer to things such as the escalator and the New York Subway PATH system. The Subway PATH had actually been destroyed in the events of September 11th but had since been rebuilt. Surveillance security cameras and security guards were notably visible everywhere. This made my brother and I very conscious in terms of our reasons for being there for a research visit, and we thought that this may make it difficult for us to take photographs of the surroundings. However, no one questioned us about taking a few photographs with a single lens reflex camera. The theme of surveillance and being watched reminded me of work by Joyce (2002) where he has written about how we present versions of ourselves in publicly acceptable ways when we know that we are being watched.

I have mentioned previously in this chapter the idea of creating detourned maps. After completion of the Ground Zero psychogeographical dérive and when we had returned back to the United Kingdom, I went about merging the New York map with the Bangkok map. An example of this map can be found in an extended account of this dérive (Bridger, 2011, 450). The map is intended to create a disorienting reading of place and represents something of the disorientating nature of psychogeographical research. The scar type pattern in the centre of the map is meant to represent where the World Trade Centre once stood but now as Ground Zero was a blackened and empty space.

The Ground Zero dérive was important in terms of developing a fully laid out account of how to conduct psychogeographical psychological research. The process enabled me to formalise how to document such research and how to write it up in academic peer-reviewed contexts. However, the project not only highlighted the failure of words to articulate personal and political response (Frosh, 2002) but also suggested new ways in which the visual, sensory, embodied and auditory worlds can be considered in relation to psychological research. It should be stated that the work that I produced whilst living in Manchester was also informed by many discussions and psychogeographical explorations with friends and colleagues such as Bob Dickinson, Mark Rainey, Morag Rose, Geoff Bunn and Steve Hanson in the Greater Manchester area. The walks and talks often took us to places such as the Northern Quarter, East Manchester, Oxford Road and the side streets off Deansgate. Many of the Manchester psychogeographers in the early 2000s went onto to form the Loiterers Resistance Movement, which now runs first Sunday of the month walks. In my psychogeographical activities in Manchester, I organised several walks and psychogeographical activities including a time capsule project, the Lunar Water Walk and general dérives in the city centres of Manchester and Stockport. It should be noted that the focus of this work was on psychogeographical investigations in the city centres of Manchester and Stockport and not in suburban or rural areas. However, one walk led by Phil Smith did lead its participants from the city centre of Manchester to the countryside. That particular walk provided an interesting experience of walking from the city to the countryside with all its differing affective sights, sounds and smells.

At this phase in my work, I began involvement in organising an international festival and conference about psychogeography with academics, friends and allies. This conference and festival was named as TRIP, which stood for *Territories Reimagined: International Perspectives*. It was around this time that I was nearing the end of my PhD and I had accepted a lecturing post at the University of Huddersfield. I raise this point here as it had important implications in terms of how I was viewed by others as a 'psychogeographer'. Once I had taken up a lectureship at a university, this seemed to irrevocably change how people would view me from outside of academia. In the next part of this chapter, I will discuss my role as a psychogeographer having moved from being a student and activist of psychogeography to being labelled as an academic psychogeographer. The label of academic psychogeographer is important because with it comes an accusation that one cannot be radical and political if doing psychogeography from within a university institution. There is of course value to such an argument, but what I want to do in the rest of this chapter is to explain how it is important and necessary to continue to do radical and critical work not only in the university but outside and beyond it.

Huddersfield

The next phase of my work that I will discuss is my Huddersfield work, where I have conceptualised psychogeography as a feminist psychological approach, and more recent work, where I have developed psychogeography as a participatory research approach to working with people with mental health needs and with people identifying as or as allies of LGBTQ+. The academic work has coexisted alongside my work outside of academia, which has included attending and organising dérives and talks in Huddersfield and other towns, cities and villages for the Leeds Psychogeographical Group, the Huddersfield Psychogeographical Network and the 4th World Congress of Psychogeography. I have also been involved in creating further fictional characters and groups beyond the Bored in the City Collective, which has included the character of David Bollinger. The final part of this chapter will include a discussion of the fictionally based academic war research group, Perudi.

Having written in this book about developing a psychogeographical psychological approach via the dérive at Ground Zero, I now move onto discussing my work on conceptualising a feminist approach to psychogeography, which is based on a paper written for the *Feminism & Psychology* journal (Bridger, 2013). Much of the previous situationist, geographical and psychogeographical work has taken a masculinist focus. Gillian Rose (2003, 137) has explained that 'various white, bourgeois heterosexual masculinity have structured the way in which geography as a discipline claims know space, place and landscape'. Doreen Massey (1984, cited in Women and Geography Study Group, WGSG, 1984, 13) has indicated that, 'a feminist analysis in the broadest sense is one done from an anti-sexist perspective and can be concerned with any subject'. Indeed, some ex-situationists such as Ralph Rumney have indicated that many of the members of the Situationist International held quite sexist views in relation to what men and women should and shouldn't do. Furthermore, other ex-situationists such as Michèle Berstein have explained how their contributions as women in the Situationist International were not always fully acknowledged:

> One of the curious things about the IS (sic) was that it was extraordinarily anti-feminist in practice. Women were there to type, cook supper and so on. I rather disapproved of this. Michèle has been an extraordinarily powerful and perceptive mind which is shown by the fact that she is among the most important literary critics in France today. A lot of the theory, particularly the political theory, I think originated with Michèle rather than Debord, he just took it over and put his name to it.
>
> *(Rumney, 2010, n.p.)*

This statement is important to consider in order to begin working out what a feminist approach to psychogeography and situationism should look like. Such criticisms have also been levelled at those who have developed their own psychogeographical approaches in the form of creative writing and travel books. Cultural geographer Bassett (2004, 403) discussed Iain Sinclair's psychogeographical work and explains that, 'The city appears as something feminine, passively there for the taking, a wilderness like space of adventure to be conquered or possessed'. Indeed, other feminist, lesbian and critical psychologists have challenged such heteronormative and sexist views, and they have conceptualised anti-sexist and gendered approaches to psychogeography. Here, that notably includes groups such as Precarias a la deriva (2005), Grup de Lesbianes Feministes (2005) and Burnett et al. (2004). The first group is important in terms of drawing on elements of situationist theory in relation to critical examination of women's experiences of home, work and leisure environments and the use of dérives in such places and spaces. The second group known as Grup de Lesbianes Feministes is important to consider in terms of their activist art and theatre work in public spaces such as central Barcelona and how they seek to challenge the notion of 'consumer-market subjects' and that public spaces should be used as a 'political space for collective creativity based on new forms of social, sexual and affective relations' (2005, 109). Finally, the work of Burnett et al. (2004) is important to consider here in terms of how they used the practice of the dérive to 'break' away from everyday routines of work, parental responsibilities and other commitments. These examples demonstrate new and different ways in which psychogeographical work can be done as well as the different formats that it may take, ranging from academic writing to theatre, art and activist work from a feminist perspective. This previous work has informed my approach to feminist psychogeography as I will now expand on.

There are two key concepts that can underpin a feminist psychogeographical approach and this includes embodied subjectivity and heteronormativity. Indeed, Gill (2008, 40) argues that subjectivity is gendered. Brown et al. (2007, 2) explain that 'sexualities are geographical'. In my work, I make the case for social spaces and places as being gendered and that it is necessary to investigate social relations as gendered relations. The process of moving through different environments is also an embodied experience, and it is important to consider this in psychogeographical research. My approach builds on work developed in human geography and feminist studies (i.e. Binnie and Valentine, 1999; Brown et al., 2007). The second concept to discuss here is heteronormativity. Waitt et al. (2008, 782) explain that, 'heterosexuality is always assumed to be the benchmark against which other sexualities are measured or compared'. Knopp (2004, 123) argues that the world is 'heterosexist'. Such dominant assumptions of sexuality shape, limit and constrain other forms of gender and sexuality. A critical psychological approach to environment can thus be used to counter and problematise such dominant assumptions and perceptions.

This brings me to consider what research questions and aims would underpin a feminist psychogeographical approach. Here I draw on the questions from Khatib (1958) in relation to conceptualising a psychogeographical approach. These questions informed the study that I undertook at Ground Zero (Bridger, 2011), but in the context of developing a feminist psychogeographical approach, the questions focus on a gendered mode of investigation as indicated below, as also presented in this paper (Bridger, 2011, 291):

- What are my gendered experiences of specific environment? Are these places that I would ordinarily visit? Why/Why not?
- What are the emotional and behavioural effects of familiar and unfamiliar environments?
- How do men and women enter and exit environments?
- Are there noticeable behavioural and emotional differences when moving between different environments?
- What changes need to occur within environments to facilitate possible social change?

These questions inform my feminist psychogeographical approach. Also important to consider is reflexivity and one's gendered subject position in the research process. Here, I refer to Gills's (2008, 40) arguments on 'gendered subjectivity'. I consider myself as a male feminist arguing for gendered equality. I do not claim to know what women's experiences are. Indeed, Brown (2007, 218) explains that there is a need for 'male femininities' where men could call into question gendered inequalities. The feminist approach to reflexivity indeed informs much of the underpinning basis to reflexivity in qualitative psychological research. Kimmel (1998, 60–61) explains that 'feminism provides both men and women with an extra-ordinary powerful analytical prism through which to understand their lives and a political moral imperative to transform the unequal conditions of those relationships'. To conclude this subsection of the chapter, the case is made for a feminist psychogeographical approach with a consideration to how such an approach can contribute to existing work on the areas of geography, psychology and feminist studies. Key research questions and aims are identified with a gendered reflective approach in research. An argument is made here for developing further anti-sexist methods and approaches in psychology. As Lavery (2009, 55) explains, the aim 'is not to deny men the ability to walk the city, but rather to transform patriarchal attitudes to women so that cities become truly democratic spaces'.

This previous work then moves us towards more recent research where I have taken a more applied, social, health and participatory focus. I go on to discuss here a participatory-based research project with service users at a mental health drop-in centre (Hoot) in Huddersfield. Having done solo and group derives, I was keen to think about how such work could be drawn on to do community-based psychogeographical research. However, there were initially particular difficulties in formulating such an approach in terms of it being considered initially as sessional activity work and not as community-based critical research. The task was to make it both. Three main aims of the work were initially to conduct community group work to create contributions in and out of the university, to draw on a psychogeographical approach to challenge everyday life in consumer capitalist society and to think about the extent to which political and personal changes could be advanced via such an approach. Other sub aims of the work were to work in a sustainable and collaborative manner with our partner organisations, with our research participants as well as with the general public and academic colleagues. The particular project with Hoot drew on the metaphor of 'tracing spaces' in order to trace ourselves, our research and our participants into a project about mapping spaces and their experiences of difference places and spaces. The project emerged through a creative collaboration with Emmanouil, a senior lecturer in architecture at the University of Huddersfield. She made links with the Hoot Art and Health Organisation (www.hootcreativearts.co.uk/en/index/a1 and with Out of the Blue (OOB), with the aims to make real some intentions for psychogeographically informed walks, some exhibition work and also the production of various artistic maps, poems, creative writing and other sessional activities such as yoga. Hoot and OOB are organisations located in the town of Huddersfield, which are open to the general public as well as to adults with mental health needs and learning difficulties. Part of our aims with engaging with Hoot and OOB was to make an impact outside of the university sector. We wanted to draw on our subject-specific knowledge of architecture, critical psychology, community psychology and psychogeography. Having read the works of other community-based, participatory and case-based research (Hodgetts and Stolte, 2012), we wanted to develop such an approach in community-based work with groups that would also contribute to extending the pantheon of social psychological and qualitative research in psychology.

Part of the point in working at Hoot was to push us to think about the artistic elements of psychogeographical practice and how that could connect with the people using that space on an everyday basis and how we could make the psychogeographical activities interesting and relevant to them. An important ethical theme underpinning the work is to ensure that we as the researchers worked with and not on the participants. We did not conduct structured interviews or Likert-type scale psychometric questionnaires on the participants as the aims were not to mechanically extrapolate what might be in peoples' heads. However, neither were the aims to assume that it was possible to phenomenologically get at the essence of peoples' experiences. We drew on an approach that combined critical psychology, community psychogeography and psychogeography. A community critical approach (Kagan et al., 2011) was important in terms of the ideas of social justice, stewardship and the importance of community. Hodgetts and Stolte (2012) have written about case-based research in order to think through the relations between participants and researchers to foster positive social relations. Ethics, criminal records bureau checks and risk assessment documentation were completed by Sophia Emmanouil in collaboration with the management team at Hoot.

Collaboration is thus crucial with those in and outside academia in order that, 'we use our own academic position to transform the cultural practices that we participate in' (Parker, 2015, 7) so that we can start to create new connections of our work to political praxis. Hodgetts et al. (2014, 164) quite rightly state that, 'We need to embrace the long history in psychology of working in partnership with communities to challenge inequitable social structures and to effect change'.

In the Hoot study, we deliberately set out to position ourselves as 'scholar-activists'. It was therefore important to think of our roles as academics in relation to other roles that we had. We drew linkage with other qualitative, participatory and community research (Hodgetts et al., 2010; Hodgetts and Stolte, 2012) and also other community critical and health-based research (Kagan et al., 2011). We distinguished our work from other community critical and health research by being informed by the work of the Situationist International and psychogeography. The aims of the situationists were to critique consumer capitalism not only in a playful but also political manner, and we wanted to retain that ethos in the work that we did at Hoot. Such a stance thus made it theoretically and practically distinct from other sessional work by volunteers at Hoot.

Thus the work at Hoot was underpinned by particular situationist principles, which were psychogeography, participatory creativity, detournement and provocation. In Barbrook's (2014/2015) recent book, *Class Wargames*, he wrote that those main principles can be used to challenge the current order of consumer capitalism and to begin in thinking about a world beyond a capitalist order of things. As mentioned before, the aims of the work at Hoot were not to use a method in practice but rather to consider the idea of ludic practices and gaming strategies as a way to consider environments and what needs to change in everyday spaces and places. Thus, the plan was to involve Hoot and OOB participants to take part in participatory means of understanding themselves, others and social contexts. The first concept referred to here is that of psychogeography, which has previously been defined in this book as:

> Psychogeography could set for itself the study of the precise law and specific effects of the geographical environment, consciously organised or not, on the emotions and behaviours of individuals.
>
> *(Debord, 1955, n.p.)*

The point then of doing psychogeographical activities was to politically and playfully investigate how environments may consciously and subconsciously affect us. Pinder (2005: 4) explains that, 'chance encounters and uncanny resonances could disrupt dominant ways of seeing and potentially reveal the marvellous buried within the everyday'. I wanted to draw some connection here with Freire's (1970/1993) ideas of conscientisation in relation to arguing for self-directed grassroots activism as opposed to leader-led movements. Debord never actually formulated a methodological approach to doing psychogeography and neither did he wish for himself nor did he wish for the principles of psychogeography and situationism to enter the pantheon of academia. However, there is a sense of the therapeutic value of psychogeography in what Sadler (1999: 80) indicates next about how psychogeography could be, 'regarded as a sort of therapy, a fetishisation of those parts of the city that could still rescue drifters from the clutches of functionalism, exciting the senses and the body'. However, the aims of the project at Hoot was not to deliver therapy as we were not trained therapists and it would be a conflict of role in any case to do so.

The second concept used in this particular project was that of participatory creativity, which is about how people can work together and in self-determined ways to produce new conditions for everyday living. This was a principle that underpinned how we worked at Hoot as will be explained a little later on in this chapter.

The third concept that we drew on in the project work was that of detournement. Detournement is a means by which elements of 'text' are used again in new ways to challenge the accepted order of how things are so as to create new alternative meanings (Situationist International, 1959). What I mean by 'text' here is similar to the idea put forward by Parker and the Bolton Discourse Network (1999) whereby it refers not only to the spoken and written word but also anything including images, advertisements and television programmes.

The fourth concept to be discussed here is that of provocation, which relates to an ultra-left notion of political agitating that is designed to make people able to create social changes. There are many examples of political agitation including the banners used during the events of May 1969 such as, 'Be realistic. Demand the impossible!'.

We made sure to keep to the principles of Hoot and OOB during all stages of the project. Both those organisations focus on the arts, music and creative writing (poetry, song, etc.) as a means to enhance peoples' well-being and mental health. There are many types of sessional activities taking place there including electronic music production, film making, photography, art, yoga and dance workshops. The aims of Hoot and OOB are to bring together people from all walks of life to build confidence, to encourage creativity and expressiveness and to help people find their own voices. Hoot and OOB also aim to support people to flourish and to build community relations. The participants involved in our study were of different ages, fitness levels and ability and had been referred by mental health services in relation to mental distress and anxiety.

It was of course important to build relations with the participant group at Hoot and OOB before launching our project with them.

One of the core aims of such work was to instill trust and good relations between people. Neither did we as the project workers wish to simply jet in to do research with the group and then to simply leave. That would not be fitting with the principles of social justice and working sustainably. We, as the 'project workers', wanted to work with sensitivity, ethically and creatively with the participants. Therefore, for the first few months, Emmanouil took part in many different sessional activities run by volunteer workers at Hoot. She also worked with many key staff members at Hoot to ensure that the planned psychogeography activities would fit with the ethos of the organisation and with what participants would hope to be involved in. It was also important to adhere with the ethical principles at the university, and we gained ethical approval from the Art, Design and Architecture Ethics committee. Before the study began, Emmanouil provided potential participants with information about the project including how long and where the project would take place, how the 'results' would be disseminated and what would be the potential benefits to being involved in the study. We wanted to make absolutely sure that we would not simply go to Hoot and tell people what to do. Instead, we wanted to create activities that would build on what they had already taken part in, which would also draw on giving our knowledge within respective academic contexts to the participants and also hopefully increase participants' mental and physical well-being. Staff members at Hoot and OOB were provided with the aims and objectives of the project via a workshop presentation provided by Emmanouil, which was then approved by both groups. Risk assessment documentation was also duly written up prior to the commencement of activities at the Hoot centre. The planned workshops were advertised at the Hoot centre. The activities took place both in the Hoot centre as well as in the neighbouring sidewalks and canal footpaths. The metaphor of traces again was important here in relation to creating traces of activities, which would then form part of an exhibition of work at the Huddersfield Art Gallery. In order that the activities would be properly underpinned by a 'situationist' framework, inspiration was drawn from work produced by Khatib (1958):

- What does it feel like where you walk?
- How do you engage with your surroundings?
- Do you notice any notable changes in the ambience?
- What do you think of the environment?

- What do you think needs to be changed in the environment?
- What should the environment look like?

Khatib's (1958) work was related to that particular project primarily in terms of the practice of psychogeography and with the idea of exploring the effects of environments and with what changes need to occur to change the consumer capitalist ordering of such places. Thus, the aims are not to simply explore how we feel about being in particular places, but rather the aims are to critique environments with a view to conceptualising what a non-consumer capitalist society could look like (Situationist International, 1961). By sharing these concepts and principles with participants at Hoot, we aimed to ensure that we would not positions ourselves in opposition to or as 'experts'. The point of such 'situationist' group activity was to enable each of its members to participate creatively and in a self-determined manner to consider what sort of world they want to live in. The themes that we, as the project workers, thought that could underpin the sessional activities included: consumerism, privatisation, social control and surveillance (Bridger, 2014). Using non-academic language was also very important so as not to potentially alienate anyone.

The workshops were split into five different themes decided on by Emmanouil and Bridger as: (1) Spirit of Place, (2) Sculpting Paths, (3) Dice Walk, (4) Scavenger's Hunt and (5) Map Making. Before we began each of the workshops, we started off with some relaxation activities involving yogic movements. Many members of Hoot and OOB would already have been familiar with the practice of yoga. Such activities aimed to create a relaxed environment and to form a base for what would follow. After the relaxation exercises, participants were then briefed on what activities would follow and what the rough instructions would be. However, the instructions were designed with situationist principles in mind, so participants could feel free to subvert or go against the instructions, if they so wished.

At that point, many members of Hoot and OOB were familiar with Emmanouil as she had been taking part in activities at the centre with the participants for quite a few months.

The first workshop involved considering the sense and spirit of place, and participants were asked to reflect on how they had journeyed from their homes to the Hoot centre. The first workshop took place wholly within the Hoot building and that was also intentional as it was a place that participants would be familiar and at ease with. Various sights, smells and encounters with strangers were discussed by participants. They also discussed what they wore and how they felt about going into and out of places such as the bus terminals. Following the discussion of these reflections, we asked the participants to write their experiences on a blank paper in a free associative manner. In order that they could do that, we asked them to not stop and think about what they would like to write but rather to write down the first things that came into their heads and not to cross anything out. We also suggested to them that they could highlight particular words that might have had significance to them. The participants used black marker pens to write words on Post-it notes and affixed these notes onto photographs that they had previously taken. Some of the participants also wrote poems and other creative accounts, which they discussed with others in the group. Later on, the participants and staff members at Hoot and OOB would decide which materials to exhibit at the Huddersfield Art Gallery.

The second workshop was focused on the idea of creating sculpture paths. After the participants had been briefed on what would be involved, we went out on a walk and collected objects that would form sculptural exhibits. Objects could include anything that was safe and clean to pick up and reuse. We thought that the act of picking up objects related neatly to the situationist idea of the dérive:

> Dérives involve playful constructive behaviour and awareness of psychogeographical effects, and are thus quite different from the classic notions of journey or stroll. In a dérive, one or more persons during a certain period drop their relations, their work and leisure activities and all other motives for movement and action, and let themselves be drawn by the attractions of the terrain and the encounters they find there. Chance is a less important factor in this activity than one might think: from a dérive point of view, cities have psychogeographical contours, with constant currents, fixed points and vortexes that strongly encourage and discourage entry into or exit from certain zones.
>
> *(Debord, 1958, n.p.).*

Many participants appeared to be drawn to particular objects encountered on the walk. We found certain items and then stored them in small bags provided by myself and Emmanouil. Once we had completed the walk, we went back to the Hoot base where we chose which of the items would work well as sculptural pieces. No criteria were presented as to what the sculptural exhibits should look like or where they should be placed. We then took photographs with iPads of the sculptural exhibits, and we created short accounts of where we had found the objects and why we had put together the exhibits in the ways that we had done so. This was all done in the spirit of other academic work by colleagues such as Hodgetts et al. (2007, 2011) where he discusses giving cameras to participants and with the importance of creative collaborative relations between participants and researchers. He also rightly acknowledges the importance of being transparent in giving voice to participants in such work.

The third workshop involved doing a dice walk, which involved the same members who took part in the second event. The aim of this workshop was to use the dice to take ourselves out of the routined means by which we would ordinarily get from 'a to b' in Huddersfield. The technique of dice walking lends itself well to the situationist ideas of detournement, participatory creativity and the dérive. The reasons being that the dice would be used as an anti-navigational device to disorientate ourselves in Huddersfield and to treat the surrounding environment like a giant board game where we would all take part in a critical exploration of the town. In order to make the dice a proper anti-orientational device, we affixed directional markers onto the dice so that where the number one was meant to be, we placed a direction such as 'go straight on', and where the number two should be, we placed a direction such as 'take the second left'. After we had observed and followed through with each instruction of the dice, another member of the group rolled it to indicate where we should go to next.

The fourth themed walk a few weeks later involved doing a scavenger hunt with the same participants taking part once again. Similar in many ways to the sculpture path walk, we went wandering outside of the Hoot centre down the canal footpath and surrounding sidewalks and collected numerous items of interest such as wild plants, driftwood, coins and buttons. The basis of the scavenger hunt was informed by S. Smith (2008) where he has used the process of aimless walking to get out of the routinised ways in which we may move through different spaces and places. Such work arguably connects with situationist principles of play as being political. As a group we decided when we had collected enough items and then walked back to the Hoot centre. We put the items we had found into jars, made tags to label the jars and then wrote short stories about how we had found the items and why we had decided to exhibit them. Then we went back to the Hoot centre. Most of the participants who had been involved in previous workshops came to this last session. Emmanouil and I explained at this last session that we would be writing short stories and creating artistic maps of the walks and activities that we had done. The session began with putting pen to paper to write short reflections on the walks and then sharing and commenting on what each participant had written to each other.

The fifth and last session took place two weeks later and involved creating artistic maps of the various walks and activities that had taken place in previous workshops. Most of the participants again attended this session. The idea of creating art maps of places was a practice drawn on by some members of the Situationist International including Debord and Jorn (1957). One of the maps that Debord and Jorn constructed involved piecing together how working-class people moved from one district to another in inner-city Paris. They basically cut up maps of the city and then rearranged the elements of the map to make clear how working-class people moved from place to place. Similarly, in this last workshop, Emmanouil and I encouraged participants to cut up photocopied maps that we had brought with us in order to create maps of their own. We brought maps of Huddersfield and of other towns and cities across the world as well as quotes by the situationists. Participants were encouraged to try out cutting and pasting quotes, map features and images to create artistic maps. Such practices connect with the situationist practice of detournement, which involves using pre-existing elements being reordered to create new meanings. What emerged from this final session was the idea of gentrification as well as memories of places that participants recounted and ideas for what the town could look like in the future. The focus devised by Emmanouil and I was to encourage participants to think about what Huddersfield could look like under non-capitalist conditions. The work of Khatib (1958) was drawn on to inform the sessional approach. We engaged in some interesting discussions about those themes during the course of the session.

The final layering of tracing spaces involved considering how to bring together all the artistic outputs by participants to feature in an exhibition at the Huddersfield Art Gallery. The exhibition was part of the annual series of Rotor exhibitions (www.transdisciplinarydialogue anddebate.com. Clearly, we ensured to gain consent from participants in terms of which outputs to exhibit in the gallery space. This also involved gaining ethical approval from the Management Team at Hoot and OOB. At the opening launch night, several members from Hoot attended, including Terry Barnes who gave a short talk about the potential exclusiveness of art and how it may not be accessible to everyone. He explained that the work produced by Hoot participants aimed to break down some of those boundaries and was an example of participatory art. Arguably, Terry's talk could be viewed as a type of situationist provocation as he had used the space of the art gallery to critique the institution of art itself. A nod here could be made to arguments produced by Hodgetts et al. (2011) in terms of a need for anti-expert positions and for promoting non-experts in research and practice. The workshops that we had delivered had worked to create dialogue between people across many different social, cultural and political contexts, in what was hopefully in the vein of situationist participatory creativity. Doing the psychogeographical community groupwork in various settings including the workshop space of Hoot, walking along the canal and on other footpaths enabled a great range of discussion and debate about place, history and consumer spaces. We as a group discussed gentrification in Huddersfield, memories of place, the mental health system and even hobbies and interests such as critical psychology, art and music.

Following the completion of the project, Emmanouil and I gathered feedback and testimonials from the participants. Feedback included that the sessions were: 'un-expected and the instructions given helped us to change perspective, made us feel creative and push our boundaries'. Other participants said that the workshops were: 'enjoyable', 'fun', 'innovative', invigorating', 'inspiration', 'playful and interesting' and 'nothing similar to what they have done before'. One person even said that the act of using dice got them to change their perspective on things. Another participant noted that the workshops enabled him to 'discover a different kind of creativity' and that it had let him 'unleash a lot of emotional and personal stuff' and had helped him in terms of 'reflecting' and in terms of 'mapping' their life. Such feedback certainly points to the therapeutic potential of psychogeographical activities. Another person said that the sessions had helped her in terms of 'overcoming the initial challenges of the tasks was rather fulfilling'. The participatory effects of doing a group dérive were also highlighted:

> 'From the moment we stepped out, our mind was collecting ideas, we had a collective mind and awareness was increased. We

> felt we were leaving our mark. We felt like we were pushing our boundaries, creating events within events within events. We had a trigger to be creative and have fun'.

Another participant noted that he had gained the 'tools and skills to work with in future projects'.

As well as gaining feedback from the participants, Emmanouil and I decided to conduct a go-along interview to reflect on our roles as research practitioners in the spirit of work by Kusenbach (2003). Neither of us had utilised the practice of a go-along interview before though it seemed like a useful endeavour in order to trace the routes that we had wandered through during the project and to reflect back on the work we had done in and around Hoot. I had also devised some preset questions in the vein of a semi-structured interview approach, and we discussed areas such as: our dual roles as academics and as sessional workers, ensuring that everyone felt included and involved in the project and what the impact of the work would and could be. We reflected on how the activities had the effect of 'changing their perspective on things' and that it had also 'changed the way they look at the town, Huddersfield town'. We were surprised that some of the participants had indicated that they did not wish to go near to the centre of the town as they didn't feel that it was a welcoming place. Emmanouil and I therefore ensured that we did not go near to the centre of the town during the project activities. It was pleasing that the theoretical underpinnings of situationism and psychogeography had filtered through into the responses and outputs produced from the project work and that the four situationist concepts of psychogeography, participatory creativity, detournement and provocation had been put into practice.

This then brings us to considering the conclusions of doing psychogeographical community groupwork and to the important themes of traces, legacy and the principles of social justice and sustainability. In the United Kingdom, academics based in institutions are increasingly told to evidence the public impact of their work and to engage with the wider community outside of academia. However, such pointers are often interlinked with the need to hit key performance indicators and to evidence one's research outputs and to generate research funds to justify one's role. It was our aim with this work to show how public engagement can be put into practice in a psychogeographical way. Our attempt at public engagement here was to engage and critique the principles of neoliberal consumer capitalism and to enable participants to think anew what sort of everyday living conditions that they would like and what they would like their hometown to really be like. As far as is known, situationist psychogeography does not tend to inform project sessional work though there are some clear benefits to such work as has been evidenced in this chapter. It is my aim to do future group work with communities outside of academia and to put into practice the ideas and principles from areas including situationist psychogeography, architecture, critical psychology and other disciplines such as human geography, feminism and politics. However, psychogeographical community group work does not in itself create radical social change and neither does simply writing about such ideas create change. Plant (1976: 76) makes important arguments about radical academics replicating the 'appearance of revolutionary critique while similarly reproducing the specialization of knowledge and the lucrative elitism of their roles'. Guy Debord and other situationists were against the idea of turning their ideas and theories into academic knowledge. It is of course important to consider the potential elitisim of academic roles and how such work can produce alienated forms of knowledge. It is therefore necessary to produce work that subverts, questions and detourns academia and the work produced within that context. By academics drawing affiliation with other artists and activists is one way to work in, outside and beyond the confines of academia (Aitken et al., 1996).

Group activity can also facilitate the 'self-realisation' of individuals (Vaneigem, 1975, 186–199), and these sorts of realisations can possibly lead to situations where radical social changes can take place. Indeed, Wark (2011) explains that situationst theory has the potential to help us make more sense of scenarios and groups such as occupations of space by the Occupy Movement in London and New York as well as ongoing banking crises and the Eurozone crises. Žižek (2011) also points to the importance of a critique of the consumerisation of built environments. Parker (2007) also explains that for society to change that everyone must work in and against the places and systems in which they live, work and play within. Such psychogeographical community group work thus raises important questions in terms of the sort of work that we may go about doing whether that be in academia or other contexts. This brings me to discuss a particular psychogeographical LGBTQ+ study.

Qualitative, social and community psychological research has taken a decidedly spatial turn in recent years as evidenced by the focus of work by scholars including Bridger et al. (2019), Dixon and Durrheim (2000), Hook (2007) and Reavey (2011). Our particular interest as a group of academics, artists and activities that identified as or were allies of LGBTQ+ communities was to consider this project as a critical space for creative conscientisation as well as to consider the current socio-political gendered order of things in society. This aim then sets apart such work from mainstream social psychological inquiry in studying peoples' inner attitudes and behaviours. The aims of this work then require a different methodology and approach to research in working with participants and the important relation to public spaces and gendered spaces.

Our aims were to work in a participatory way with people identifying as LGBTQ+. We wanted to carry out a walking-based research project to enable people to discuss the topics of sexuality and gender in relation to where they live, work and play. We also wanted to show people how a 'psychogeographical' approach could be used to think about everyday places and spaces and how we could think through these environments as gendered. The premise of the study went beyond simply attempting to understand and make sense of peoples' immediate experiences and feelings about spaces and places.

What we mean by psychogeography is a way of making sense of everyday places with a view to creatively imagining what an ideal arrangement of environments could look like. The seed of the idea for this project came from Gomersall who wanted to put together a qualitative project focused on the topic of sexuality and gender that would draw on a psychogeographical methodology. Gomersall formed a research team of academics with specific expertise in psychogeography (Bridger), sexuality and gender (Munro) architecture, art and design (Emmanouil and Powell). We decided that we wanted to carry out a project with people identifying as LGBTQ+ and that we would arrange a series of psychogeographical walks followed by an exhibition of photographs and text, which would be collaboratively produced by the participants and the research team. The spirit of the project was meant to be participatory, and we did not wish to create a context where the researchers would be seeking to extract data from its participants. That would be contrary to what we wanted to do as we wanted to make the power relations as equal as they could be in such a study whilst also recognising that there were distinct power relations in terms of the positions that we took within the research project, i.e. researcher, academic, artist and participant. We also wanted this study to be an example of public engagement work, and so one of the project aims was to create an art exhibition that would be showcased in Huddersfield and where the participants and research team would work together collaboratively. The formation of the research team also meant that we would all make distinct contributions based on our knowledge and working practices from subject areas including critical and community psychologies, architecture, art and design as well as sociology and gender studies. The psychogeographical focus of the study would also be informed by a participatory and community psychological agenda (Hodgetts and Stolte, 2012).

One of our key theoretical starting points was to adhere to the arguments by Hodgetts et al. (2010, 287) in terms of not simply assuming that places are just 'backdrops to social processes'. Rather than wanting to investigate the social processes between people in relation to environments, we wanted to explore dialogical accounts between people in the walking group about sexuality and gender. The way that we wanted to work with people in this project meant that attempting to observe peoples' inner attitudes or their external behaviours in relation to places would not work well with our research questions.

We decided to label this study as focusing on the LGBTQ+ community because this comprised the range of people identifying under that category within this project. We used a critical community psychological approach (Kagan et al., 2011) as we wanted to foster and develop the relations between the project team and the participants. We took inspiration from the work of Parker (2015, 7) where he writes about how we need to 'use our own academic position to transform the cultural practices that we participate in' so that we can build connections between academics and the everyday world. Hodgetts et al. (2014, 164) also raise a very important point about how 'we need to embrace the long history in psychology of working in partnership with communities to challenge inequitable social structures and to affect change'.

The label of scholar-artist-activist was also important to this project. It was important for us to think through our social roles as academics in relation to working with the participants. Such work can never be totally balanced in terms of power relations though we endeavoured to reflect on our roles in the project and to consider how that shaped whom we were working with. We took heed of arguments produced by other similarly based scholar-activists such as Hodgetts et al. (2010), Hodgetts and Stolte (2012) and Kagan et al. (2011). However, we also wanted to build on that work by making links to the work of the situationists. Whilst the situationists were not academics, their work has been drawn on by many people from within academia (Richardson, 2015; P. Smith, 2015; and Wark 2011). We decided to draw on the work of the situationists because they had conceptualised a walking-based approach to study everyday environments. Moreover, they did not just wish to simply understand peoples' experiences of environments but rather they aimed to understand such spaces in order to begin to envision an alternative order of things in society. Their aims were revolutionary as they wanted to create radical social change rather than simply to understand how things are or to re-explain how things were in society. We took heed of arguments by Vaneigem (1975, 186–99) where he explained that being in a group is meant to enable the self-realisation of each person and that these realisations are meant to lead people to create social changes in their everyday lives as well as in society.

The aims of this study were not simply to run sessional walking activities as would ordinarily be run in day centres, but rather that the activities were threaded through with a situationist approach and informed by our practices from psychology, sociology, art, design and architecture. In using a situationist approach in this project and in line with previous studies undertaken by members of the project team, we drew on key concepts from the work of Barbrook (2014/2015), which included psychogeography, participatory creativity, detournement and provocation. These concepts were intended to provide strategies and ways to critique gendered capitalism. Some members of the project team were somewhat ambivalent about the use of a methodology in the study given its connotations with experimental psychology, positivism and treating people in research as 'subjects'. We drew on notions of gaming and art-practice within the design of the project. The first concept of psychogeography was the main approach used within this project. Debord, a leading member of the situationists, provides a useful definition of psychogeography:

> Psychogeography could set for itself the study of the precise law and specific effects of the geographical environment, consciously organised or not, on the emotions and behaviours of individuals.
>
> *(Debord, 1955, n.p.)*

We take this definition by Debord and we see the value of exploring the effects of environments on our emotions and behaviour. Debord's definition does seem somewhat similar to that provided by environmental psychologists and social psychological understandings of place from the 1980s. However, in the work of Debord and the situationists, they sought to playfully and politically explore their everyday environments in order to critique capitalism and to consider an alternative order of things. Pinder (2005, 4) talks about the importance of deconstructing the mainstream ways in which we understand environments and says that we should do this to see the 'marvellous buried within the everyday'. However, criticisms have been raised of the situationist approach to psychogeography and subsequent proponents of that approach due to grounding in the male gaze (Bridger, 2013). The second concept that we drew on in our study was that of participatory creativity. As mentioned earlier in this paper, we did not wish to instate a dichotomous relation between the project team and the participants. Instead, we wanted to create environments where we could all work in participatory ways with each other to walk, talk and produce various 'objects of knowledge' such as an exhibition of art, public presentations, academic talks and several peer-reviewed academic articles. The third concept that we drew on in this project was that of detournement. Detournement refers to deconstructing dominant text and image and re-ordering such things so as to create subversive and alternative readings for its audiences (Jorn, 1959). We aimed to create detournment in the project by exploring ways to question taken for granted assumptions about how we might navigate everyday spaces and places as well as thinking about social spaces as gendered spaces. The fourth concept drawn on in this project was that of provocation. Provocation is a concept commonly used by people in ultra-left groups and examples and can include agitating the middle to upper classes and calling for a revolution. This can be seen in the attempts by the Parisians in the 1950s and 60s where some groups called for radical social change and chanted ideas such as, 'Be realistic! Demand the impossible!'. We would try to create situations of provocation in the study in order to question taken for granted assumptions about social spaces and places. It should be noted that there is some degree of overlap with these four concepts. We draw on these four concepts in explaining the project work in the next section of this paper.

Before we started contacting potential participants, we sought ethical approval from the ethics board at the University of Huddersfield.

All of the project team worked at the University of Huddersfield and many of the participants identifying as LGBTQ+ were lived and/or worked in Huddersfield and so it made sense to host the first walk in the town. For the other walks we wanted to go further afield than Huddersfield and so we decided to undertake walks in other towns including Batley and Holmfirth. The project team wrote a leaflet providing information on the four walks, and the aims of the project and the leaflets were distributed at local community centres and libraries in and around the Huddersfield area. Gomersall also went to a local LGBT group in Huddersfield and spoke about the project to its members. Several of the group members expressed interest in being part of this project, and so they were then provided with info and invited to the four walks. We decided on different psychogeographical walking techniques for each of the walks, and part of the reasoning for that was to create interest and diversity for those involved. Further information relating to the rationale for each of these walks will be provided later in this paper. The walks were underpinned by a paper by Khatib (1958), where he outlines key questions that can underpin psychogeographical investigations. We also took guidance from another research group, which provides a blueprint for how to do to feminist psychogeographical research (Bridger et al., 2017, 47):

> What does it feel like where you walk?
> How do you engage with your surroundings?
> Do you notice any notable changes in ambience?
> What do you think of the environment?
> What do you think needs to be changed in the environment?
> What should the environment look like?

The form of the wording above looks initially similar to a phenomenological reading of environments though the focus on 'what do you think needs to be changed' provokes a potentially more critical and subversive analysis, i.e. understanding capitalist environments in order to change them and also understanding hetero-patriarchal environments in order to change them. We drew on the questions listed previously here when we conducted the four walks for this project. The 'practice' for each of the walks lent itself to the situationist use of the dérive:

> Dérives involve playful constructive behaviour and awareness of psychogeographical effects, and are thus quite different from the

> classic notions of journey or stroll. In a dérive, one or more persons during a certain period drop their relations, their work and leisure activities and all other motives for movement and action, and let themselves be drawn by the attractions of the terrain and the encounters they find there. Chance is a less important factor in this activity than one might think: from a dérive point of view, cities have psychogeographical contours, with constant currents, fixed points and vortexes that strongly encourage and discourage entry into or exit from certain zones.
>
> *(Debord, 1958, n.p.)*

The practice of walking draws on many human senses including sight, sound and ambulation. In order to capture some key aspects of the walk, we decided to take photographs. Hodgetts et al. (2007, 2011) explain that providing cameras to people in project work is a useful way to create dialogue and to foster good relations between researchers and participants. We therefore borrowed cameras and MP3 players from the technicians at the University of Huddersfield. A participatory and non-hierarchical focus was central to each of the walks. This was important to the project team because the walks were meant to be led by its participants rather than the researchers and we wanted everyone to feel as included as they could be. However, we did also acknowledge that power relations can never be fully flattened out and that we were there in the capacity as researchers with participants. We reflect on the idea of power relations and subject positions in the conclusions to this article. The four walks took place in Huddersfield, Batley, Holmfirth and Manchester Canal Street. The first walk took place in Huddersfield because this was where the majority of the project team and participants lived and worked. It made sense for the first walk to take place in this location because of its importance as an everyday space for all involved in the project. Batley and Holmfirth were chosen for their differences in type of location with Batley as a small industrial town and Holmfirth known as a leafy and peaceful village. We chose Manchester for the fourth walk given its status as a hub for the LGBTQ+ scene with Canal Street and also because we thought it would be nice for the project team and participants to venture further afield than their local environments. The choice of Manchester Canal Street for the final walk as a city walk was considered as a different enough focus from the other three locations. There was also a seasonal focus with each of the walks with the Huddersfield walk taking place in June, Holmfirth in July, Batley in August and Manchester Canal Street in October.

The first walk was also the launch date for the project and those participants who had expressed interest in being involved attended as well as the research team. Before the walk commenced, the research team introduced and explained what the project was all about and then this was followed by a briefing on what would be done on the first walk. For the first walk, we had decided to do a dice walk dérive as this is quite a creative and playful way to experiment with the surroundings and to turn the idea of a walk into a game. The purpose of this game was to be focused on understanding public space as gendered space, to take us out of the routine ways in which we would ordinarily walk from 'a to b' in the town and to 'detourn' and open up how we would affectively respond to public spaces. The dots on the six-sided dice were removed and replaced with directional instructions such as go straight ahead, turn left, turn right, take the second right, take the first left and turn around. We had decided that once each instruction had been obeyed a new participant or member of the research team would roll the dice to decide where we could go next. We used a big soft dice so that this could then be rolled onto the streets and it would thus keep with the idea of treating the town as a giant gaming floor.

During the first walk, Marcel indicated that he liked using the dice to walk around Huddersfield because 'it's quite cool … and you don't actually have to go to the places that you think you might want to go. You just go where the dice takes you'. This reflection fitted with the creative and game-like nature of the walk and also with the random possibilities of what dice walking can enable understanding social spaces and places in new and different ways. It was then a *querying* and *queering* of space as we were aiming to understand the space of the town. Once we had walked for about an hour and a half, we were all somewhat tired and so decided to conclude the proceedings by going to a local public house in order to discuss our thoughts and reflections on the walk and to have a social drink. Much of the discussions focused on historical gendered reflections on Huddersfield town, what once was and what was now, i.e. an old pub that had now been turned into a car park, as well as broader discussions about gender and sexuality, i.e. London moving the Pride March to Huddersfield in 1981.

The second walk took place in August in Batley, and there was no particular plan for the walk other than to begin in the centre of the town and to wander outwards to the outskirts of the town. Much of the discussions on this walk centred around the lack of financial investment into the town and also talking about the sad news about the then recent murder of local Labour MP Jo Cox. The third walk took place in Holmfirth in September. There were many more people who attended this particular walk, and so we split in to four groups of approximately six with the aim to do a scavenger hunt. Scavenger hunts are often done by artists and poets with the aims to collate lost objects in order to create sculptures to be photographed and then presented in exhibitions or art portfolios. The ideas for this walk also drew on the work of S. Smith (2008) in terms of the practice of wandering and walking as a way to break with routinised patterns of being and thinking. On introducing the plan for this particular walk, there was no criteria imposed as to what people should collect and create. People on this walk collected items such as flowers, notes, wrappings and small toys. Before each group set off on the walk, the research team instructed the groups to return after one hour to the Holmfirth Picturedrome with their sculptures. What was particularly interesting about this walk was that participants did not really bring up the theme of social spaces as gendered spaces. The theme of nature and the environment was a particularly prominent theme of this walk, though this was also accompanied by discussions about what young people do in the local area. For example, one participant commented that,

> A policeman did tell me that there was more of a drugs problem in Holmfirth and other posh areas than in more stereotypically deprived areas because the kids have got a lot more money and they can get it from Mummy and Daddy.

Another participant commented in response that, 'We found the wild side of Holmfirth, As you know, parks everywhere…it was obvious what young people want to do…things that their parents would not approve of'.

The fourth and final walk took place in Manchester Canal Street. The starting point for the walk was the Thomas Edison statue on a bench at location X. From there, we walked over to Manchester Canal Street. As it was by now late October, the night was drawing in quite quickly, and this turned into a night walk that yielded a very different ambience than the other three walks in towns and the country. The theme of social space as gendered space was a prominent theme on this walk though added to this was the idea of gentrified queer spaces and the problems with the hetero-sexification of Canal Street with the rise of stag and hen parties.

The first action following the walks was to present an exhibition in a public local space. Originally, we were going to submit a proposal for our exhibition to the Huddersfield Art Gallery. We decided that the best place to exhibit the work would be as part of the Temporary Contemporary exhibition in the Queensgate Market https://research.hud.ac.uk/art-design/temporarycontemporary/. It was important to the ethos of this project that such an exhibition be accessible to as many people as possible. The location of the Temporary Contemporary exhibition in the Queensgate market meant that people who might not ordinarily go to exhibitions would see the work that we had created. This seemed a better fit of our project with the space of the market. The Temporary Contemporary series is a partnership with the School of Art, Design and Architecture at the University of Huddersfield, the traders in the Queensgate Market and Kirklees Council (Markets and Creative Economies Team). The series is a space in which artists, businesses, academics and students can showcase their work. We found out about a call for exhibition proposals for the Market Showcase, which is part of the Temporary Contemporary series of exhibitions. The Market Showcase enables local artists, businesses, academics and students to present their work in unoccupied stalls in the Queensgate Market. The project team submitted an exhibition proposal to the curators of the Temporary Contemporary team, which was positively received and then accepted. We then decided as a project team as to what the exhibition would look like and what photographs and text to include. Participants were invited to two exhibition planning meetings, and some of the people involved in previous walks selected some photographs and audio to include in the exhibition. For many of the photographs, we chose to overlay the photos with key accounts provided by the participants and project team. We decided on this action because we wanted to direct viewers to think about the images of places in particular ways. Whilst it is not possible to control how people make sense of the images of places, it is possible to direct people to the ways in which they might understand such texts. We also wanted to overlay key images with text so as to question some of the taken for granted ways in which we might make sense of spaces and places, i.e. rethinking the roles of superheroes as not necessarily having to be heterosexual. There are very few superheroes who are not heterosexual though this is beginning to change with the representation of transgender characters such as 'Switch' in the film, *The Matrix*. However, attendance to the exhibition planning meetings was quite low with only a few of the participants joining in. When we put together the artefacts for the exhibition, we ensured to include peoples' contributions as well as anonymise those peoples' work where they had indicated their request to not be named. There was a launch in the evening for the exhibition, which attracted local interest amongst local artists, academics and the general public. The exhibition ran for several weeks and appeared to be a success. One particular attendee at the exhibition launch night commented very favourably on the exhibition and stated that they thought it made an important, creative and useful contribution to thinking about LGBTQ+ issues in the local area.

Other outputs produced from this project included an LGBTQ walk for a public run culture, creativity and community conference at the Lawrence Batley Theatre in Huddersfield (February 16, 2018), a summary of the project at the 4th World Congress of Psychogeography (September 7, 2018) and a presentation at the academic Spaces and Flows conference in Heidelberg in Germany (October 25, 2018). We wanted our project to have local, national and international impact and recognition.

By drawing on key concepts including psychogeography, participatory creativity, detournement and provocation enabled us to do more than simply going for a walk into different places. This chapter has aimed to show a range of ways in which to put into practice key concepts to enable new and useful ways in which to do psychogeographically informed community and applied social psychology research.

One cannot underestimate the potential of psychogeographical walking to be a positive force for health and well-being. This was particularly apparent during the walk in Holmfirth where many participants enjoyed the therapeutic aspects of walking in the countryside as many of them did not generally go beyond the town of Huddersfield to visit the Moors and wider surrounding countryside. Psychogeography has been viewed by other writers as a type of therapy, as argued by one writer who views it 'as a sort of therapy, a fetishization of those parts of the city that could still rescue drifters from the clutches of functionalism, exciting the senses and the body' (Sadler, 1999, 80). It was indeed a key aim that the psychogeographical walks would enable those involved to feel a certain freedom from 'functionalism' and capitalism, though we hadn't expected the walks to have therapeutic value. As for whether the psychogeographical walks led to 'consciousness raising', we are not all that sure as that was not something captured in MP3 recordings nor in any discussions.

There were particular challenges with writing this work in a way to connect it to a gender informed community and applied social psychological approach. The participants and project team attended most if not all the walks and meetings. It helped that so many of the project team and participants were able to come to most of the walks as it meant that we could develop familiarity and sound working relationships. However, not many of the participants were able to attend the planned meetings for the exhibition showcase. One participant indicated that they would have liked to have been more involved in the planning of the exhibition and writing up of the work but because of the short timescale that they ended up with it made it impossible for them to contribute. There is something here of a challenge in terms of the academic fast-slow way of working and a dissonance with non-academic ability to be involved in this type of work. Finding better ways of working across academic and non-academic contexts is something we have become more aware of and which we will more fully consider in future projects.

This work and other outputs produced from the project are also primarily a production of the academic research team and not the participants. Whilst the participants voices are presented in this paper and other outputs, the academic papers and presentations are productions of the research team. This then inevitably puts the voice upon the research team to tell the story of their participants. In future work, we would like to expand and put into practice better ways of involving our participants in writing, exhibiting and communicating projects to various audiences.

During the process of the research project, GDPR regulations came into force. This meant that we had to adjust some of our working practices and how we used participants' data in the study. The research team had collected a sizeable amount of data including photographs, MP3 recordings and diary notes, and so we stored such material on the University of Huddersfield's approved 'K' drive and not on cloud servers such as Google Drive and Dropbox.

There needs to be further development of psychogeographical projects, exhibitions and other outputs. There is certainly a need for this type of work in Northern towns and cities including Huddersfield, Batley and Manchester. The form of towns and cities changes rapidly, and it is important to do theoretical and practical-based work to understand local and global spaces and places. With seemingly more divisions between people on racial, cultural and gendered levels, it is more important than ever to do work that brings people together across the boundaries. This work has also served as what is hopefully useful engagement activity. Since the completion of this work, further psychogeographical work has been undertaken in Huddersfield, including future planned work with other colleagues in the university, the continuation of the 4th World Congress of Psychogeography and the use of a shop space in the Market Hall in Huddersfield, i.e. a pop-up psychogeography 'shop' space. We see such work as a useful way to bring people together to talk about social spaces as gendered spaces, and it has been useful to bring people together from a range of different vantage points, i.e. queer, hetero, pan, bi, academic, artist, activist, and so on. We hope that this work can usefully inform and extend the pantheon of community and applied social psychological research.

Playwriting

Psychogeography has no place in psychology or at least that is the argument put forward by some psychologists. The same argument could also be made for the role of 'play' in academic work in that play also has no place in psychology or in the acceptable work of psychology academics in university departments. However, in the next part of this chapter, I will explain and outline how a focus on playwriting and play can be an important part of psychogeographical academic work. In this next part of the chapter, I take a turn away from the standard convention of writing for peer-reviewed publications in order to explain why and how a playwriting approach to psychogeography can be deployed both in and beyond the world of academia. In this next part of the chapter, I reflect on my role in working as an academic in a psychology department in the United Kingdom and how a neoliberal order of things shapes the ways in which theoretical work can and cannot be done.

I want to consider here the male character of John Nada, in John Carpenter's film, *They Live.* At this point, I want to make a connection of psychogeography with the work of De Certeau (1974/1984) and to Barthes' (1972) approach to semiology. De Certeau (1974/1984) wrote about the idea of walking as a way of reading and decoding environments, and as he argued, 'walking affirms, suspects, tries out, transgresses, respects, etc., the trajectories it "speaks"' (1974, 99). The work of De Certeau (1974/1984) is of relevance here in terms of the idea of getting a bird's eye view of built environments from the top of skyscrapers in New York city:

> the ordinary practitioners of the city live down below, below the thresholds at which visibility begins. They walk – an elementary form of this experience of the city; they are walkers, Wandersmänner, whose bodies follow the thicks and thins of an urban "text" they write about without being able to read it.
>
> *(De Certeau, 1974/1984, 93)*

The practice of doing psychogeography lends itself well to 'top-down' and 'bottom-up' approaches. Psychogeography does not approach things in a monodirectional manner but rather deploys multiple lines of travel: left, right, backwards, forwards and turning around.

Let me return to the film example of Carpenter's film, *They Live*. The narrative of the film is seen through the eyes of the main character John Nada. At the start of the film, Nada is presented as a homeless working person wandering the streets of Los Angeles. The act of wandering is akin to the situationist idea of the dérive, and by chance he finds himself in an empty church and discovers a box full of sunglasses. This doesn't initially seem like much of a discovery until Nada puts on a pair of the sunglasses and then starts to wander the streets. To his surprise, he doesn't see the advertisements that he would be accustomed to view such as advertisements for Coca Cola, mortgage offers and holiday products, but instead, he reads instructions to 'Obey', 'Consume' and 'Conform'. He suddenly reads the signs of the city very differently, and the experience is somewhat similar to a Barthes (1974) position of moving from a citizen position as a consumer with 'false consciousness' and not seeing the world as it really is, to a citizen position as an anti-consumer with enlightened consciousness and freed from the shackles of capitalist attitudes and its behavioural effects.

Slovenian psychoanalyst Slavoj Žižek (2013) undertook an analysis of the said film, in his own film, *The Perverts Guide to Ideology*, where he indicates that Nada's sunglasses function as 'ideology glasses' that

> allow you to see the real message beneath all the propaganda, publicity and posters. You see a large publicity board telling you to have a holiday of a lifetime and when you put on the glasses you just see on the white background; a grey inscription.

Žižek makes the case that the trashcan signifies a particular type of ideology and that to eat from the trashcan means that one actively consumes ideology. The rubbish in the trashcan thus symbolises the objects, or what could be referred to as the products of capitalism. Žižek also argues that, 'when you put the glasses on, you see dictatorship in democracy. It's the invisible order, which sustains your apparent freedom'. He explains that ideology is the 'spontaneous relation to our social world, how we perceive each meaning and so on and so on. We in a way, enjoy our ideology'. Arguably, the pleasure in the ideology is the thing that needs breaking; however, when something gives a sense of pleasure, it is challenging to break such habits – though this is what the situationists attempted to achieve through the practice of the dérive and in drawing on other tactics such as provocation and detournement. The challenge of breaking the link between the pleasurable feelings and the ideology is articulated in the film via a confrontation between John Nada and his close friend John Armitage. Nada tells Armitage to put on the sunglasses and Armitage's response is, 'I don't wanna fight ya. I don't wanna fight ya. Stop it. No!'. Then shortly afterwards, Nada replies, 'Put on the glasses'. This would appear for Armitage as, what Billig et al. (1988) would refer to as, an ideological dilemma. Žižek argues that the reason why Armitage refuses to put on the sunglasses is because this is meant to represent the idea that he refuses to accept the imperatives of the capitalist system and that to accept such conditions would be too painful and distressing for him to accept. This then poses an interesting question for audiences to consider in terms of whether they too wish to live in the 'lie' of capitalism or whether they choose, like Nada, to don the sunglasses in order to expose the realities of capitalism. Žižek (2013) explains that Carpenter's film serves as an important example of 'Hollywood Left' film production. The critique of capitalism embedded in the film is of course a central mantra of situationism with the aims to 'critique urbanism' (Debord, 1955) and to overturn capitalist society. Carpenter's film was set within the Reagan years and can be considered to be a criticism of consumer capitalism, conformity and commercialisation. It is important here also that instructions such as 'conformity' and obeying are seen not as attitudes that just exist in peoples' heads and that can be observed via experimental psychological studies but instead in this film are exposed and read as signifiers that construct particular coded meanings within capitalist society.

Carpenter's film is an important one that can be connected with fictional psychogeographical characters to form part of a new critical psychological approach or even an approach beyond critical psychology and psychology.

Parker (2015: 7) explains that there is a need to create 'practical interventions in discourse by those outside of discourse analysis'. In his book, he refers to an example by the London Psychogeographical Association (LPA, 1997), where they drew on the idea of three-sided football matches in order to 'free people from the shackles of dualistic thinking' (LPA, 1997, 88). To what extent could academic thinking reinforce dualistic thought? A refusal here by the LPA to engage with the typical parameters of intellectual thought, which is usually connected with and then assimilated with academic is one way to do such work. Here then, the LPA refuses to engage in a typical mode of academic argument, and where they want people themselves to decode, subvert and overturn the symbols of capitalism. Parker (2015) also explains that, 'how we, on this side of our boundary, will use our position in solidarity with them and how we will use our own academic position to transform the cultural practices that we participate in' (Parker, 2015, 7). One possible way to transform the cultural practices that we participate in is to transform how we present ourselves through the written word vis-à-vis via fictional characters, as will shortly be explained.

What would John Nada's experience of walking through a city in the Western world look like today? If say, he knew what he knew about consumer capitalism back in the United States during the Reagan years, then what would an American city or, say, a Western European city look like now? I'd like to pose the scenario here of John Nada, walking around the city centre of Manchester in 2018 and by considering what he might see if he were to put on the special sunglasses. Many of the advertisement instructions might indeed look quite similar in terms of imperatives and instructions to obey, consume and conform. However, some of the images may appear more muddled with the spectre of fake news plastered over the billboards. Moreover, Nada would also probably have a smartphone, which also would be a medium for communicating other advertisements to him such as subscribing to dating apps, foam mattresses and durex condoms.

What would Nada's sunglasses reveal to him in terms of what is now considered as 'fake news'? In Debord's (2010) later work, *Comments on the Society of the Spectacle*, he writes about how capitalism continues to reinvent itself and that social activists and those on the left (i.e. situationists) need to continuously change tactics in order to combat spectacular capitalism. I agree with Debord's sentiments here and would argue further that one must continue to draw on the metaphorical use of sunglasses in order to read the symbolically loaded signs and symbols in towns and cities. John Nada is in essence a psychogeographer, and his role in the film is arguably that of an anti-hero of capitalism who is tasked with encouraging others to challenge the spectacle of capitalism to lead to its eventual downfall.

There is useful work within the area of critical psychology that can be drawn on to further discuss the role of fictional identities and in terms of developing playwriting as an alternative form of theoretical knowledge that can produce useful insights for critical psychology and psychology as a discipline.

Writing in the voice of 'an-other' person, i.e. a fictional character, can alter the way in which one writes in academic and non-academic contexts. In the mid-1990s, a group of critical social psychologists wrote under the pseudonym Beryl Curt and published a book called, *Textuality and Techtonics: Troubling Social and Psychological Science* (Curt, 1994). The writers involved with Beryl Curt included: Chris Eccleston, Kate Gleeson, Nick Lee, Wendy and Rex Stainton Rogers, Paul Stenner and Marcia Worrell. In that book, they argued that the aims of using the fictional character of Beryl Curt to write about critical psychology 'was an attempt to find ways-of-writing-about ways-of-working' (Stainton Rogers and Stainton Rogers, 1997, 45). This raises a very interesting question about how to make sense of the ways in which we work and how to develop alternative modes of writing and expression in academia. One of the benefits of writing under the rubric of a collective voice is that it can enable a questioning of the authority of the academic voice, and in the context of this subject area of psychology, it can enable one to question the orthodoxy of psychological science and the hypothetic-deductive approach. I found the work of Curt (1994) to be a fascinating read in terms of how they used a collectivist voice to think through how they write and critically approach disciplinary knowledge and that inspired me to invent the fictional character of Dr. David Bollinger.

I have used the character of David Bollinger to think through the productive effects of power relations, neoliberalism in the context of academic working conditions, Brexit negotiations and the return and rise of cognitivism in UK psychology departments. The use of writing in fictional characters into academic work would seem at first glance as a bit of an anomaly and not really considered as appropriate or correct. Indeed, when considering the ways in which academics are assessed in terms of their research at UK institutions via the Research Excellence Framework, they have to submit several of their own papers and be able to demonstrate a percentage contribution to such work. When one considers the possible use of writing under pseudonyms, this then makes that process of reviewing academic's work rather more complicated. However, there are important reasons why one would want to write under a pseudonym or even carry out research or critical work under the guise of a different person, as will be explained here.

One psychogeographical intervention in my workplace involved constructing an office space for David Bollinger in the Department of Psychology at the University of Huddersfield. In a recent wave of office moves across the university campus, the Department of Psychology moved from the Ramsden building to the Edith Key building. In the flurry of all the moves, I subverted my office door name from just including me to including 'Dr David Bollinger' and that my office was the 'Institute for Psychogeographical Studies'. Bollinger had his own desk in the office along with a brown corduroy suit jacket draped over a chair. Several colleagues passed by the office and thought that a new member of staff had been appointed though they soon realised that the person was a fiction! One colleague in particular warned me of the risk of creating fictional narratives and that under the new academic climate a disciplinary could follow. Another colleague indicated that writing under a fictional name would 'not be REFable' (Anon, 2017). Bollinger in a sense became a medium through which to understand the borders and boundaries of values and ideas in a psychology department in the current era of neoliberalism and austerity. It is probably also important to acknowledge the alter ego element of creating fictional characters through which one writes 'through' and about.

Bolly as an alter ego

Dr. David Bollinger has been constructed as a leading figure of post situationist theory and who has emerged onto the psychogeography 'scene' in September 2017. At the last *4th World Congress of Psychogeography* in September 2017, Bollinger had his first 'outing' where he entered into debate about the current problems of academic, activist and artistic psychogeography with another fictional leading character called Fenella Brandenberg, played by schizocartographer and cultural theorist, Tina Richardson.

Now I discuss a theatrical performance involving Bollinger and Brandenberg. The play was loosely based on J.G. Ballard's (1974/2011) *Concrete Island*. Psychogeographers are often drawn to Ballard's work because of the way in which he documents human relationships amidst the backdrop of urbanism and dystopian narratives. Richardson and I decided to draw on this play for a performative piece at the *4th World Congress of Psychogeography* on the September 4, 2019 at the University of Huddersfield. We chose this particular book of Ballard's because we found it of interest in how the lead character, Maitland, was stuck on a motorway 'island' and couldn't escape. In some ways, this seems eerily similar to the lockdown conditions facing citizens across the world during the COVID-19 pandemic, where we are all facing having to 'stay at home' and 'stay safe'. However, in drawing on Ballard's story about *Concrete Island*, we did not simply wish to replicate the novel. We wanted to rework the content of the story and weave in new threads into the narrative. Therefore, we decided to do a dérive at the Trafford Centre and then to write that account into a new version of Ballard's *Concrete Island*. Whilst on dérive at the Trafford Centre, we took photos and made notes of our critical observations about consumerism and shopping. However, doing a dérive at the Trafford Centre is actually quite difficult to do in practice because the structure of the site only allows one to walk in a linear manner from one end to the other in both the ground and first floor levels. The only real areas for dérive possibilities include the food quarter in the middle of the Trafford Centre and within each shop. However, we did manage to dérive in an 'in-between' area of the Trafford Centre, which was undergoing new development with new commercial and retail space. Once we had concluded the dérive, we accidently got lost in the Trafford Centre car park, and this turned out to also be part of the dérive and we had inadvertently become like Maitland, Sheppard and other characters in Ballard's *Concrete Island* novel who had become marooned on a motorway embankment, albeit in our circumstances, we were trapped in the Trafford Centre car park with no way to get out until we could find the car to take us all back home. The 'real' dérive therefore took place at the end of the walk. The following transcript is a reworked adaption of Ballard's novel *Concrete Island*. The play is based on an email exchange between Richardson and Bridger, where we took on the roles of Sheppard and Maitland, with other characters being included such as Charlotte Tillbury, 'Mini' David and Guy Debord. The following transcript was read out by Richardson and Bridger at the *4th World Congress of Psychogeography*:

THE ISLAND

STARRING JANE SHEPPARD, ROBERT MAITLAND, GUY DEBORD, THE TRAFFORD CENTRE, THE TRAFFORD CENTRE CAR PARK, MINI DAVID, CHARLOTTE TILLBURY, FENELLA BRANDENBURG, GUY DEBORD AND THE B&Q ON THE B5211

JS: Rest try not to move. We've sent for help. You are on Trafford Island, injured. You are lucky that you are still alive. You have been drifting in and out of consciousness, muttering about your car. We have called an ambulance and they will be coming soon. Don't move, keep still and we will take care of you till the ambulance arrives.

RM: (Maitland lifts his head up. He is visibly dazed and confused) Are we … are we in the Trafford Centre car park? Which car park zone are we in? I crashed my car … my Renault … I went off the motorway, of the verge and rolled the car into the Trafford Centre car park … but there are a lot of car parks here … I can't seem to orientate myself that well … where am I? Is an ambulance on its way?

JS: You're quite safe, Mr. Maitland. The ambulance is on its way. We're near the Trafford Centre car park. Don't worry about your car. Just rest. You talk to yourself all the time. You confuse me when you talk about the car park and your car. I bought you here. You're damned heavy you know.

RM: Where is here? It looks like we are in New Orleans in a café. (Maitland feels the sweat on his head and looks at this hands). Oh my God … I need a doctor! I can give you money. Help me onto the road and we can stop a car. How much money do you want? My wallet … it's in the car, in the trunk. I can give you fifty pounds.

S: You are too ill to be moved. Don't worry about your car, it is still in the car park, we can find it later. You need to sleep. You are safe here on the island. Sleep now…and dream of Greek Goddesses, or balmy New Orleans nights and the sound of jazz bands.

RM: Are we on an island? This is all quite confusing! I've got to get to a hospital. My leg needs looking at. My colleagues at the 4th World Congress of Psychogeography, my wife, my son David … they will wonder where I am.

JS: But they think you are away on a business trip and are probably not missing you at all. Forget that psychogeography lot at the Fourth World Congress, we will take care of you. Those bimblers won't be able to help you. They don't know the Trafford Centre like we do.

RM: You told me that you called the police last night. Did you? Will you help me get out of here? I don't even know what day it is.

JS: We can't call the police. Debord is terrified of them, this is the only place he's got. The police haven't been so welcoming of his graffiti in the past and stirring up the workers and students. When they built the Trafford Centre, they sealed him in. All last night you were mumbling, Mr. Maitland, calling out for your wife and asking for Fenella.

RM: Jane, I want you to call Debord right now. You and Debord can carry me up the Barton embankment and leave me there. I'll be able to stop a driver.

JS: I don't know how to get you there. I don't know the area that well. I don't really live here. I'm staying with some friends near the B&Q on the B5211.

RM: Ok Jane! I'm not going to call the police! I won't report you or Debord. I'm grateful to you. If you hadn't have found me, I could have died here. The breakdown men won't give a damn about anything around here. I can give you money if that is what you need?

JS: I don't want anything from you. You're the one who needs help! Let's face it, you're really unhappy with your life, especially your wife…and that Fenella women, too, so it seems…

RM: (Maitland avoids Jane's fierce gaze and pulls himself along the wall to the doorway. He steps towards the doorway and looks out at the outside world. Everything seemed larger, more contoured, a maze of roads and car parks. The vegetation on the grassy verges was wild and lush, as if the Trafford Centre was moving back or forwards in time to a pre or post urban capitalist environment).

The messages that I wrote. Did you wipe them off?

JS: Debord did. He wiped them off and then wrote in their place "Beneath the car park, the beach".

RM: (The scent of Jane's body contrasted with the smell of the grass and car exhaust gases. Maitland sat down on a truck tyre on the ground. He gazed up at the high wall of the motorway embankment. The newly seeded grass was growing more densely on the surface. Soon the grass would hide all traces of his accident, the deep ruts left by the tyres of his car, the confused marks of his struggle up the embankment. Maitland felt a brief moment of regret on leaving the Trafford Centre. He would have liked to preserve it forever, so that he could bring his wife, son and friends to see this place of an ordeal).

Jane …

[…]

JS: Wake up. Are you alright? Wake up! What have you done to him Debord?

RM: (Maitland stretches out his crab like hands. He grabs Jane's hand in a fierce manner).

I've decided that I want to stay in this car park. I want to do a car park dérive like that fellow Gareth Rees. Maybe it will be a dérive with no end … a continuous dérive! Where is Debord? I need to talk to him.

(The sleep had refreshed Maitland and he was beginning to feel calmer and clearer).

JS: Your leg is looking better. You were nearly walking this morning. I think you could perhaps cope with a small dérive around the car park. I could contact either Gareth or Kevin Beresford for advice. But why do you want to stay and why here with Debord?

RM: A small dérive of an hour or two would be fine but it should be followed with a continuous dérive! There is much wrong with today's contemporary capitalist world and its necessary to do a total critique of urbanism to lead to new social conditions and society. Debord can help me with that mission.

(Two hours later and Maitland was sitting in the small shack, a pavilion of rust which Debord had built around him with discarded sections of car parts. Maitland sat comfortably in the shack and watched with satisfaction as Debord completed the last assembly. Debord had brought in beds for everyone and Maitland thought that this was comfortable enough to live in and fitted with his views on a sustainable anti-capitalist world).

JS: Debord's done a good job. Far better than most of the speculative building that's going up these days around here. I can see you are a real architect, Mr Maitland. This is definitely not a winner of the Carbuncle Cup, like Redrock in Stockport. Are you going to spend the night here?

RM: No – this is my summer house. Debord has built another residence of a more permanent nature for us all to live in within this car park.

(Maitland takes the bottle of wine from Jane and raises it to his lips. Like a mendicant desert chief presiding over his barren kingdom, he squatted on the bed. He had gone beyond exhaustion and hunger to a state where the laws of psychogeography had been suspended. He listened to the traffic outside).

JS: Debord is still waiting for his wine. You're not going to leave here. Let me tell you, you're not. You imagine you can just lie here thinking about unitary urbanism all day, dreaming of a futurist utopia where functionality meets ludicity. No-one gives a damn what you think. You – you're no-one!

RM: (Maitland drifted away from her, dimly aware of her voice drumming through the darkening air. He was convinced that his body was no longer absorbing anything he ate or drank – the wine had formed a cold lake within his stomach).

JS: (Jane struck his face with her hand, trying to hold his attention) I think you're a lousy middle-aged creep and I'm not going to follow your lunatic psychogeographical ideology. Who do you think you are? Constant Nieuwenhuys. This isn't the New Babylon! You're demented!

RM: (Maitland put his hand where Jane had slapped him on his face. He looked at Jane and appears shocked and outraged).

I am the alpha and omega of psychogeography. You, however, are a traitor to the tradition of psychogeography!

JS: You are rambling again, Mr. Maitland. You humiliate me with this kind of conversation. You are a deluded man. You know the Situationist project is a failed one. Thank God you will soon be out of my life.

RM: No. Shouldn't we all stay together, here with Debord, in this car park, forever? I don't want anyone else to know that I am here.

JS: A while ago you were asking for the police and an ambulance, calling out for your wife and Fenella, worrying about work. Now you want to stay here! You are contradicting yourself. Are you trying to become the Trafford Centre, absorb it via osmosis, like some form of deep topography? Making the molecules of the Trafford Centre become one and the same with your own body?

RM: Yes, I think I am slowly becoming one with the Trafford Centre. The Trafford Centre is me and I am the Trafford Centre. Each parking space forms an atom in my own body. The windows of the Trafford Centre form a window into my own soul, the windows are my eyes. And the walls and concrete of the Trafford Centre, are my skin. The shops are the various parts of my body, Selfridges is my heart, John Lewis my brain and M&S my stomach, liver and kidneys. If you want to leave, then you can, but I will stay here in the Trafford Centre car park. There is nowhere else for me to go. You and Debord should stay here with me!

JS: Debord cannot leave. He has been here since 1983, when he published *The Society of the Spectacle.* I asked him earlier what he thought about your staying here and your new 'becoming' and he said: "a society which eliminates geographical distance reproduces distance internally as spectacular separation", although I am not sure exactly if he was referring to your absorption of the shopping centre or just making some abstract comment about the spectacular nature of the shopping experience *per se.*

RM: I do not agree with Debord. What I am doing is taking situationist thought and moving it onwards in order to completely overturn situations. Revolution or assimilation, those are the only two options available today. We are in the age of the Brexo-spectacle 3.0. The practice of the dérive is not just a hobby, it has now invaded my whole sense of beingness so that as I wander around the Trafford Centre and the car park, it is me and I am the Trafford Centre. I follow no set path here, I simply wander. I let myself be drawn to the immense force emanating from this place. I plan nothing. I simply dérive. I present a total critique of situations to lead to a liberation of everyday life.

JS: Mr Maitland, Debord says "in the spectacle…the reality of time has been replaced by the advertisement of time" and what you are doing with your self-absorbed perambulatory attempt to become the Trafford Centre is to become the spectacle itself? This is the answer to your desperate life as an unsuccessful architect and the futility of your failed relationships?

RM: In order to demolish the spectacle, we have to put ourselves in the spectacle, we need to fully understand fully its machinations of power and from that position it will then be possible to overturn it and replace it with something new … something we cannot yet envisage. This is something that Debord himself said! Unless he has changed his position! It's also really hard to locate oneself totally outside of the spectacle. The spectacle makes everyone its players in a giant 'game'. We need to create new 'games', new language and new practices in order to overturn it … and then we can create something new! Living in the Trafford Centre car park has enabled me to crystallise my political views and to work out what I need to do next. I have decided that I want to stay here, I want to dérive continuously and to create a new 'science of situations'. Liberate everyday life! Fight the totality! And I want to help Debord find the beach under the Trafford Centre car park. Also, I haven't seen the Trafford Centre resident cat Emile Zola for a while. Where is he?

JS: Zola is now living in the Ocean Liner Food Hall along with a gorgeous little calico cat he picked up outside of Selfridges. They plan to make their home near the sphinxes in the Egyptian section of the shopping centre.

RM: I am pleased that Zola is alright and has found a feline friend! What happens now then? Will you and Debord remain or will you leave?

JS: I haven't quite decided yet. I am thinking of either reprising my role in the stage play of *All the King's Horses* by Michelle Bernstein, or writing a Laura Oldfield Ford inspired book called *Savage Shopping* about my time here in the Trafford Centre.

RM: I think you should get involved in both those projects here in this car park. The conditions are ideal for 'post-situationist' critical thinking and for action! Why don't you roll a dice to decide on what to do? Roll 1, 2, 3, 4, or 5 and stay here or roll 6 and leave. This should be an easier decision than that Brexit one!

JS: Staying here and performing Bernstein's book as a form of Mardi Gras in the New Orleans area of the Trafford Centre would be marvellous. And, what better place to carry on with my research on consumer culture, than here at the most Baudrillardian shopping centre in the North of England: Dumplington's very own simulacra. Perhaps we can combine our projects in some way?

RM: Yes, that sounds like an excellent idea to combine our projects. But what about Debord? Is he going to bury himself in one of the many Trafford Centre car parks?

JS: Yes! Debord alluded to a King Richard the third-esque kind of car park performance-type burial that he would like to be viewed by all those driving past on the M60.

RM: An excellent plan! As I am an architect by trade, I will create a design plan for Debord. I feel quite inspired by the Egyptian pharaohs, the Greco vases and the main spire of the Trafford Centre. But maybe Debord will live on and transcend the human body, becoming one with the Trafford Centre like me. That is what becomes of great psychogeographers and post psychogeographers.

END

The point of writing this play was to present not only a political but also a playful post situationist analysis of modern-day psychogeography as well as to consider the consumer capitalist order of things. The play could have been delivered in a very different format as a joint academic paper presentation, but we had decided to present the ideas in the format of a play so as to make the event more 'entertaining' for delegates and also to demonstrate that situationist writings need not only be considered as theoretical writings but can also take many other formats such as plays, novels and film.

Key parallels from Ballard's (1974/2011) book *Concrete Island* include:

- The main character Maitland is lost under a motorway embankment – whilst in the play Maitland, Sheppard and others are lost in the Trafford Centre car park. Fiction becomes reality as we do really become lost.
- Maitland's family in the novel – in the play, Maitland's family becomes the author's family.
- The motorway embankment in the novel becomes the Trafford Centre car park. And here we make links to Gareth Rees' (2019) book *Car Park Life*.

- Techniques for becoming 'lost' in the Trafford Centre in order to properly do a dérive – using a dice to determine where to go next.
- Situationism during Debord's leadership of the Situationist International – Situationism in the present day, cults and academia. How academic approaches and perspectives can become imbued with cult-like status and gather 'followers'. The dangers of psychogeography and situationism being absorbed into academia and of such work being assimilated into the neoliberal order of things.
- Therefore, there is a need to rework situationism in order to make it relevant and applicable for the present day order of things. Situationism 3.0 beyond situationism and postsituationism.

Wargaming

The final example that I want to refer to here is the work of a parody war research group known as Perudi, which stands for the 'Centre for People Related Research – Understanding and Influencing Human Behaviour'. Perudi presented a video presentation at the 4th World Congress of Psychogeography in September 2019. The wording of Perudi is a semantic play with the word parody and as such should be considered as both a critical, political and satirical analysis of how university academics sometimes build relations with particular organisations and nation states, which are arguably problematic in terms of the use and misuse of academic knowledge in warzones, for interrogation techniques with prisoners of war and so forth. In a recent call for papers that went out to academics in the United Kingdom in 2019, there was a call for research that could be applied in theatres of war. This is in the context where historically many university academics in the United States and in European Universities have begun relationships with organisations and where human rights groups have raised concerns with certain institutions with such relations. Perudi explained that they had responded to a Ministry of Defence Research Capability Call for Defence Science and Technology Lab Research. The focus of Perudi's work in the presentation was to make a case for an 'agile, high risk, high reward science' that could be used by the UK Defence Services. Perudi's focus was on the use of cognitive psychological research to 'shape attitudes and beliefs' and to 'enhance the human capabilities of our People for sustained growth and prosperity'. The delivery of the presentation was via a video link to YouTube (www.youtube.com/watch?v=I2sKVoGzeE4) and where the members of the group narrated the talk into a computer programme, which was presented by a robot speaking about the war research group. All the wording in the presentation made use of key words, which were accessed through a Ministry of Defence MOD presentation available online at: www.slideshare.net/LauraThompson94/dstl-human-and-social-sciences-research-industry-day-presentation

The initial response to the video by delegates at the 4th World Congress of Psychogeography was a mixture of surprise, shock and humour. At first, there were some members of the audience that did not seem quite sure as to how they should respond though people quickly realised that the presentation was a parody and critique of how academic knowledge can be assimilated by those in power and for the purposes of war and conflict.

In this chapter, I have provided a detailed layout of key exemplars of psychogeographical research. Hopefully, this account has been useful in order to demonstrate a range of different ways of doing psychogeography, which has presented it as my approach considers key elements in terms of walking, theoretical writing and playwriting. In the chapter, I have considered solo and group dérives alongside the use of taking photographs, creating detourned maps and art as well as writing up papers for peer-reviewed academic psychology journals. I hope to have extended psychogeographical work from beyond a practice of walking to consider playwriting, wargaming and strategy and also how psychogeography can be considered as a theoretical approach, subject and way of thinking about the world. Politics and play are two important axes of situationist thought and are important for considering the development of critical ideas and practice. Moreover, the point of the group-based activities in the chapter is hopefully in line with what Vaneigem (1975) argued in the *Revolution of Everyday Life*, in terms of facilitating class realisation and consciousness raising. In Chapter 4, I will discuss the implications of psychogeography for psychology and academia in general. Psychology as a discipline is very reluctant to change given its fixation on quantitative modes of inquiry and the seemingly mono perspective of cognitive experimentalism. This makes it all the more challenging to try and introduce new ideas and methods into the discipline. The challenge to change psychology is one thing but to change society is quite another thing. In Chapter 4, I discuss the idea of post psychology and what might follow in its place.The question of what place psychogeography has in psychology will be considered as will the relation of academic knowledge to society and what are the benefits of such knowledge to people and for considering the question of social change.

References

Aitken, G., Alldred, P., Allwood, R., Billington, T., Burman, E., Goldberg, B., Heenan, C., Juan, A., Lopez, G., Mark, D., & Warner, S. (1996). *Psychology discourse practice: From regulation to resistance.* London:Taylor & Francis.

Anon. (2017). Personal communications. Huddersfield.

Anon. (2020). Personal communications. Huddersfield.

Atkinson, P. (1997). Narrative turn or blind alley? *Qualitative Health Research,* 7(3), 325–344. http://doi.org/10.1177/104973239700700302

Ballard, J.G. (1974/2011). *Concrete island.* London: Harper Collins.

Barbrook, R. (2014/2015). *Class wargames: Ludic subversion against spectacular capitalism.* New York: Minor Compositions.

Barnes, T.J., & Duncan, J.S. (Eds.). (1992). *Writing worlds: Discourse, text and metaphor in the representation of landscape.* London: Routledge.

Barthes, R. (1972). *Mythologies.* London:Vintage.

Barthes, R. (1974). *S/Z.* New York: Hill & Wang.

Bassett, K. (2004). Walking as an aesthetic practice and a critical tool: Some psychogeographic experiments. *Journal of Geography in Higher Education,* 28(3), 397–410. https://doi.org/10.1080/0309826042000286965

Billig, M., Condor, S., Edwards, D., Gane, M., Middleton, D., & Radley, A. (1988). *Ideological dilemmas: A social psychology of everyday thinking.* London: Sage.

Binnie, J., & Valentine, G. (1999). Geographies of sexuality: A review of progress. *Progress in Human Geography,* 23(2), 175–187. https://doi.org/10.1177%2F030913259902300202

Bridger, A.J. (2011). Psychogeography and the study of social environments. In P. Reavey (Ed.), *Visual methods in psychology: Using and interpreting images in qualitative research* (pp. 284–295). Hove: Psychology Press.

Bridger, A.J. (2013). Psychogeography and Feminist Methodology. *Feminism and Psychology,* 23(3), 285–298. https://doi.org/10.1177%2F0959353513481783

Bridger, A.J. (2014). Visualising Manchester: Exploring new ways to study urban environments with reference to situationist theory, the dérive and qualitative research. *Qualitative Research in Psychology,* 11(1), 78–97. https://doi.org/10.1080/14780887.2012.719071

Bridger, A.J., Emmanouil, S., & Lawthom, R. (2017). trace.space: A psychogeographical community project with members of an arts and health organisation. *Qualitative Research in Psychology*, 14(1), 42–61. https://doi.org/10.1080/14780887.2016.1219799

Bridger, A.J., Emmanouil, S., & Lawthom, R. (2019). The psychogeographical turn in applied social psychology. In K. O'Doherty & Hodgetts, D. (Eds.), *The sage handbook of applied social psychology* (pp. 519–529). London: Sage.

Brown, M. (2007). Conclusions and future directions, or our hopes for geographies (and queer geographies). In K. Browne, J. Lim & G. Brown (Eds.), *Geographies of sexualities: Theory, practices and politics*. Farnham: Ashgate.

Brown, G., Browne, K., & Lim, J. (2007). Introduction, or why have a book on queer geo-graphies of sexualities? In K. Browne, J. Lim, & G. Brown (Eds.), *Geographies of sexualities: Theory, practices and politics* (pp. 1–20). Farnham: Ashgate.

Burnett, J., Cudworth, E., & Tamboukou, M. (2004). Women on dérive: Autobiographical explorations of lived spaces. In *Women and Geography Study Group, Geography and Gender Reconsidered*. CD-ROM, August: 118–141.

Butler, J. (2004). *Precarious life: the powers of mourning and violence*. London: Verso.

Chtcheglov, I. (1958). *Formulary for a new urbanism*. Retrieved from the Situationist International website: www.cddc.vt.edu/sionline/presitu/ formulary.html

Curt, B. (1994). *Textuality and techtonics: Troubling social and psychological science*. London: McGraw-Hill.

Debord, G. (1955). *Introduction to a critique of urban geography*. Retrieved from the Nothingness website: http://library.nothingness.org/articles/SI/en/display/2

Debord, G. (1958). *Theory of the dérive*. Retrieved from the Situationist International website: www.cddc.vt.edu/sionline/si/theory.html

Debord, G. (2010). *Comments on the society of the spectacle*. London: Verso.

Debord, G., & Jorn, A. (1957). The naked city map. In S. Sadler (1999). *The situationist city*. London: MIT Press.

De Certeau, M. (1984). *The practice of everyday life, Vol. 1*. Minneapolis, MN. University of Minnesota Press. (Original work published 1974)

Dixon, J., & Durrheim, K. (2000). Displacing place identity: A discursive approach to locating self and other. *British Journal of Social Psychology*, 39(1), 27–44. https://doi.org/10.1348/014466600164318

Ford, L.O. (2019). *Savage Messiah*. London: Verso.

Freire, P. (1993). *Pedagogy of the oppressed*. New York: Herder and Herder. (Original work published 1970)

Frosh, S. (2002). Enjoyment, bigotry, discourse and cognition. *British Journal of Social Psychology*, 41(2), 189–193.

Gill, R. (2008). Empowerment/sexism: Female sexual agency in contemporary advertising. *Feminism and Psychology*, 18(1), 35–60. https://doi.org/10.1177%2F0959353507084950

Grup de Lesbianes Feministes. (2005). Exploring new ways of insubmission in social representation. *Annual Review of Critical Psychology*, 1(4), 107–114.

Harley, J.B. (1988a). Deconstructing the map. *Cartographica*, 26(2), 1–20.

Harley, J.B. (1988b). Maps, knowledge and power. In D. Cosgrave & S. Daniels (Eds.), *The iconography of landscape* (pp. 277–312). Cambridge: Cambridge University Press.

Harley, J.B. (1992). Deconstructing the map. In T. Barnes & J. Duncan (Eds.), *Writing worlds: discourse, text and metaphor in the representation of landscape*. London: Routledge.

Hayes, G. (2003). Walking the streets: psychology and the flâneur. *Annual Review of Critical Psychology*, 1(3), 50–66.

Hodgetts, D., Chamberlain, K., & Groot, S. (2011). Reflections on the visual in community research and action. In P. Reavey (Ed.), *Visual methods in psychology: Using and interpreting images in qualitative research* (pp. 299–313). London: Routledge.

Hodgetts, D., Chamberlain, K., & Radley, A. (2007). Considering photographs never taken during a photo-production project. *Qualitative Research in Psychology*, 4(4), 263–280. https://doi.org/10.1080/14780880701583181

Hodgetts, D., Drew, N., Sonn, C., Stolte, O., Nikora, L.W., & Curtis, C. (2010). *Social psychology and everyday life*. Basingstoke: Palgrave MacMillan.

Hodgetts, D., & Stolte, O.E. (2012). Case-based research in community and social psychology: Introduction to the special issue. *Journal of Community and Applied Social Psychology*, 22(5), 379–389. https://doi.org/10.1002/casp.2124

Hodgetts, D., Stolte, O., Chamberlain, K., Radley, A., Groot, S., & Waimarie Nikora, L. (2010). The mobile hermit and the city: Considering links between places, objects and identities in social psychological research on homelessness. *British Journal of Social Psychology*, 49(2), 285–303. https://doi.org/10.1348/014466609X450465

Hodgetts, D., Stolte, O., & Groot, S. (2014). Towards a relationally and action-orientated applied social psychology of homelessness. *Social and Personality Psychology Compass*, 8(4), 156–164. https://doi.org/10.1111/spc3.12096

Holt, N.L. (2003). Representation, legitimation and autoethnography: an autoethnographic writing story. *International Journal of Qualitative Methods*, 2(1), 1–22. https://doi.org/10.1177%2F160940690300200102

Hook, D. (2007). *Foucault, psychology and the analytics of power*. Basingstoke: Palgrave MacMillan.

Jorn, A. (1959). *Mémoires*. New York: Wittenborn.

Joyce, P. (2002). *The social in question: New bearings in history and the social sciences*. London: Routledge.

Kagan, C., Burton, M., Duckett, P.S., Lawthom, R., & Siddiqque, A. (2011). *Critical community psychology*. Oxford: Wiley-Blackwell.

Khatib, A. (1958). *Attempt at a psychogeographical description of Les Halles*. Retrieved from the Situationist International Website: www.cddc.vt.edu/sionline/si/leshalles.html

Kimmel, M.S. (1998). Who's afraid of men doing feminism? In T. Digby (Ed.), *Men doing feminism* (pp. 57–68). London and New York: Routledge.

Knopp, L. (2004). Ontologies of place, placelessness, and movement: Queer quests for identity and their impacts on contemporary geographic thought. *Gender, Place and Culture*, 11(1), 121–134. https://doi.org/10.1080/0966369042000188585

Kusenbach, M. (2003). Street phenomenology: The go-along as ethnographic research tool. *Ethnography*, 4(3), 455–485. https://doi.org/10.1177%2F146613810343007

Lavery, C. (2009). Mourning walk and pedestrian performance: History, aesthetics and ethics. In R. Mock (Ed.), *Walking, writing and performance: Autobiographical texts* (pp. 41–56). Bristol: Intellect.

London Psychogeographical Association. (1997). Say no to the Millennium. *London Psychogeographical Association Newsletter*, 14, 1–4.

Massey, D.B. (1984). *Spatial divisions of labour: Social structures and the geography of production* (2nd ed.). New York: Routledge.

Melancholic Troglodytes. (2003). Anti-capitalism. *Annual Review of Critical Psychology*, 3. Retrieved from the Discourse Unit website: https://discourseunit.com/annual-review/arcp-3-2003/

Parker, I. (2007). *Revolution in psychology: From alienation to emancipation*. London: Pluto Press.

Parker, I. (2015). *Psychology after the crisis: Scientific paradigms and political Debate*. London: Routledge.

Parker, I., & the Bolton Discourse Network. (1999). *Critical textwork: An introduction to varieties of discourse and analysis*. Buckingham: Open University Press.

Pinder, D. (2005). *Visions of the city: Utopianism, power and politics in twentieth century urbanism*. Edinburgh: Edinburgh University Press.

Plant, S. (1992). *The most radical gesture: The situationist international in a post-modern age*. London: Routledge.

Precarias a la Deriva. (2004). *Adrift through the circuits of feminised precarious work*. Transversal texts 4. Retrieved from the Transversal website: http://eipcp.net/transversal/0704/precarias1/en

Precarias a la Deriva. (2005). Housewives, maids, cleaning ladies and caregivers in general: care in the communication continuum. *Annual Review of Critical Psychology*, 1(4), 188–198.

Reavey, P. (2011). *Visual methods in psychology: Using and interpreting images in qualitative research*. London: Routledge.

Reavey, P. (Ed.). (2020). *A handbook of visual methods in psychology: Using and interpreting images in qualitative research* (2nd ed.). London: Routledge.

Rees, G. (2019). *Car park life: A portrait of Britain's unexplored urban wilderness*. London: Influx Press.

Richardson, T. (Ed.). (2015). *Walking inside out: Contemporary British psychogeography*. London: Roman and Littlefield.Rose, N. (1999). *Governing the soul: The shaping of the private self* (2nd ed.). London: Free Association Books.

Rose, G. (2003). *Visual methodologies: An introduction to researching with visual methods*. London: Sage.

Rumney, R. (2010). *About the historification of the Situationist International: Ralph Rumney in conversation with Stewart Home*. Retrieved from the Stuart Home website: www.stewarthomesociety.org/interviews/rumney.htm

Sadler, S. (1999). *The situationist city*. London: MIT Press.

Situationist International. (1959). *Détournement as negation and prelude*. Retrieved from the Situationist International website: www.cddc.vt.edu/sionline/si/detournement.html

Situationist International. (1961). *Critique of urbanism*. Retrieved from the Situationist International website: www.cddc.vt.edu/sionline/si/critique.html

Smith, P. (2015). *Walking's new movement*. Dorset: Triarchy Press.

Smith, S. (2008). *How to be an explorer of the world*. New York: Penguin Group.

Sparkes, A.C. (2000). Autoethnography and narratives of self: Reflections on criteria in action. *Sociology of Sport Journal*, 17(1), 21–43. https://doi.org/10.1123/ssj.17.1.21

Stainton Rogers, W., & Stainton Rogers, R. (1997). Does critical social psychology mean the end of the world? *Critical Social Psychology*. London: Sage.

Thrift, N. (2004). Intensities of feeling: Towards a spatial politics of affect. *Geografiska Annaler: Series B Human Geography*, 86(1), 57–78. https://doi.org/10.1111/j.0435-3684.2004.00154.x

Vaneigem, R. (1975). *The revolution of everyday life*. London: Practical Paradise.

Waitt, G., Markwell, K., & Gorman-Murray, A. (2008). Challenging heteronormativity in tourism studies: Locating progress. *Progress in Human Geography*, 32(6), 185–207. https://doi.org/10.1177%2F0309132508089827

Wark, M. (2011). *The beach beneath the street: The everyday life and glorious times of the Situationist International*. London: Verso Books.

Willig, C. (2011). *Introducing qualitative research in psychology*. London: Open University Press.

Žižek, S. (2011). *Democracy is the enemy*. Retrieved from the London Review of Books website: www.lrb.co.uk/blog/2011/10/28/slavoj-

Žižek, S., & Fiennes, S. (Dir.). (2013). *The pervert's guide to ideology* [DVD]. New York: Zeitgeist Films.

4

CONCLUSIONS

In this final chapter, I want to cover several key areas, which include a summary discussion of the key concepts relating to the psychogeographical psychological approach (referring to psychologisation, ethics, recuperation, anti-theory and the cognitive turn); walking methods, the psychogeographical approach and psychogeography as not simply being about walking (referring to arguments on ableism, disability, methods and the psychogeographical approach) and the next steps for research in this area and moving in and beyond psychogeography (referring to arguments on post psychology and post psychogeography). This chapter ends with concluding remarks about the use and application of a psychogeographical approach in a post COVID-19 world and what a post-Chtcheglovian formulary for a new urbanism might look like.

In this book, I have provided an outline of what psychogeographical psychological research can look like. Whilst this is not a prescriptive guide or a simple tool kit, I hope that I have provided readers of this text with suggestions for how they may design and carry out their own psychogeographical studies, whether that be in psychology or more widely in the social sciences, arts and humanities or even beyond academia. Psychogeography is inherently a playful way to think and do things, and such work should be done with a view to envision new ways of envisioning the social world. Without a political critique of the neoliberal world, psychogeography potentially becomes nothing more than a way to produce self-indulgent experiences of places or

DOI: 10.4324/9781315648095-4

works just as a form of artistic expression. This is why an overtly political usage of a psychogeographical approach is key to the sort of work advocated here.

Key concepts

Previously in this book, I have discussed the key concepts that can underpin psychogeographical psychological research. In this chapter, I focus on key concepts that relate to particular challenges and issues to doing psychogeography in universities and how such concepts can 'ripple out' into everyday practices and activist praxis. I begin here with the concept of psychologisation.

Psychologisation

Psychological knowledge often comes to inform various forms of understanding human behaviour and attitudes across the social sciences, humanities and the arts. This is also the case with much of the psychogeographical work to date in relation to how such work is often done to get to the inner meanings of environments and what things really mean to human beings. However, in this work, I want to challenge the psychologisation of psychogeography and point towards an approach that goes 'beyond' such assumptions. I did not choose to become a critical psychologist only to turn back into cognitivism and the mainstream ways of thinking about human beings and social action. A psychogeographical approach should retain at its core a critique of neoliberalism and the neoliberal shaping of human experience of the focus on turning 'inwards', the cognitive paradigm and the lack of consideration of culture and politics.

Ethics

In this work, I begun a discussion of psychogeography as a walking methodology, but as argued in this work, it can encompass much more than that. Psychogeography is a theoretical approach, methodology and practice in its own right. Historically, many psychogeographers have focused on the study of able-bodied human mobility though this in itself does a disservice to those who draw on psychogeography with a range of 'disabilities'. Colleagues such as Rose (2015) are working on the development of such approaches in their work and future psychogeographical research must focus on the widest range of ways of thinking and going through social spaces and places.

Secondly, in terms of ethics, psychogeographical research places researchers and its participants or 'co-researchers' in quite different subject positions and relations of power than is typically the case in psychological research. There is no clear demarcation of researcher with participants if say both conduct a psychogeographical study in a town or a city. Where researchers work with specific organisations and groups, the relations of power and varying positions must be spoken about and discussed by all to avoid what Freeman (1972) refers to as a 'tyranny of structurelessness'. This is particularly the case in, for example, studies with participants with mental health needs in drop-in centres (i.e. Bridger et al., 2017). Researchers must avoid abusing their positions of power and must adhere to codes of conduct according to their professional affiliations (i.e. British Psychological Society) and as per their workplaces (Ethics panels and workplace contracts and codes of conduct).

As researchers, we have a duty of care to consider how we work ethically and professionally with various groups that may be considered to be 'vulnerable' or who may be considered as having mental health needs or other social and/or medical 'conditions'. It is important that we use our knowledge and training as psychologists to support those that may have a need and where necessary to refer them to other social organisations. For some people, the more immediate concerns of dealing with personal mental distress may be their focus rather than the overthrow of capitalism, and this was particularly the case with some of the participants in the Trace space project (Bridger et al., 2017). Though it is still possible to at least draw on some of the playful aspects of psychogeographical theory and practice, which may be of use to people in their everyday lives, whether that be to consumer everyday spaces and places in which they may travel or in terms of thinking about the consumer capitalist formation of environments. It is also important to consider one's position in research and in wider engagement work with the public, and I acknowledge my position as a mid-career white middle-class male with a Greek background. This position of course informs my approach to research as documented in previous published work. This then leads me into the next key concept, which includes recuperation and assimilation.

Recuperation and assimilation

To be a 'critical psychologist' in the 1980s and early 1990s was to badge oneself as a radical and socially conscious academic. However, in recent years, the badge of critical psychologist has become synonymous with mainstream psychology and with a view of mixing qualitative and critical psychological research with quantitative, cognitive and neuropsychological research. The 'mixing' of methods and approaches has led to what has been argued to be a dilution of the radical and social potential of critical psychological research. In recent years, colleagues have argued for a 'decommodified' approach to psychological and social scientific research and practice (McDonald et al., 2017). Indeed, the shift of academics from publishing or perishing has now moved to that of being only as successful as the last grant capture activity. The move from research and writing to bidding and writing as a result of research has led to an increasing commodification of the academic terrain. The nail in the coffin for UK universities was the full requirement of all undergraduate students to pay their own fees, for academics to justify their income via grant capture and to create sometimes unethical and dubious business relationships with other institutions nationally and internationally in order to stay financially afloat. All these moves have led to radical implications for the sort of work that critical psychologists can do and how they may or may not be validated within psychology departments. Many critical psychologists have left psychology departments to work in other subject areas that are more accepting of the work that they do. One could argue that we are witnessing the second evolution of cognitivism, which has had grand repercussions and negative implications for critical and qualitative psychologists. Primarily, the validation of radical and socially conscious research does not garner the same level of respectability and 'tenure' in the United Kingdom and Europe as does cognitive research, which tends to draw the big grants and related stature. Parker (2015, 7) raises an important point in terms of using 'our own academic position to transform the cultural practices that we participate in'. This point is particularly interesting to consider in terms of the position of psychogeographical psychologists and what cultural practices that they may participate in and be able to transform. In reflecting on my position in working in a psychology department, I would say that I have been able to change not very much. However, the impact of such work has had greater reach in terms of academic and lay audiences reading about psychogeography as well as public engagement psychogeography activities in Yorkshire and Greater Manchester in the United Kingdom. Psychogeographical theory and practice enables us to use our positions in academia to build alliances with people both inside and outside of university systems. Such work has enabled me to formulate new participatory ways of doing research with others as well as considering the wider social implications of research in society. Psychogeography is not something that should stay as knowledge and practice within the 'Ivory Towers' but should be something that is accessible to everyone. This brings me to my next point, raised by Parker (2007) where he explains that it is important to work in, against and beyond the discipline of psychology. Social change in any social context or society is not something that can be done purely from the 'sidelines' but is something that needs to be actioned in all areas and contexts. Sadie Plant (1992, 76), explains that, 'radical academics produce the appearance of revolutionary critique while similarly reproducing their specialisations of knowledge and the lucrative elitism of their roles'. Her argument raises several questions in terms of the extent to which the formulation of a psychogeographical psychological approach produces a specific formalisation of knowledge: Does work 'appear' simply as a false 'revolutionary critique'? Does work act to maintain my role as an 'elitist' academic? and Can one be both a 'radical' academic as well as an activist? Some people would say 'no' as any work done in academic institutions is still tied up with a neoliberal system of knowledge. However, one can strategically use the tactics of the situationists in academic working practices and research to open up spaces for contestation and refusal of the neoliberal agenda. This is maybe easier said than done as it is also very difficult to write in such a way for peer-reviewed publications, conferences and academic posts, which require a certain 'putting aside' of one's political positioning. How does one then do politically relevant work and the sorts of political 'interventions', which the situationists would have done in academic contexts? Maybe some ways of doing such work are to raise pertinent questions within one's writing, lectures and public events, to refuse assimilation and recuperation by actively deploying situationist concepts such as detournement and provocation. The liberation psychologists have always argued for the application of knowledge to create conscientisation, and this is a key idea within a psychogeographical approach – to create and enable forms of conscientisation so that others can see with clarity the order of things of society, the constructedness of things and how things and situations could be arranged rather differently. Therefore, what is being argued here is that psychogeography can be a tool amongst many other tools and knowledges to further the cause of social justice and social change. Debord (1970) wrote about the ever-increasing sophistication of the spectacle and how it was built to further the social alienation of its people. There is then a need to 'combat' the spectacle and to create ever sophisticated means in which to challenge and overturn it (Debord, 2010). In the words of the FRELIMO President Dr Mondlane 'a luta continua' which means the struggle continues. Therefore, as critical psychologists we should work analytically as researchers as well as socially and politically in our communities and in non-academic contexts. This brings me to discuss the next key concept and challenge relating to doing psychogeographical research, which is to do with anti-theory.

Anti-theory

Some individuals consider that the practice and activity of psychogeography has become too theoretical and 'academic', and they often explain that others should just do psychogeography without thinking about it too much. I would argue against such claims and would indicate that any approach, methodology or practice is always underpinned by theory and such underpinnings need to continue to be reworked for the particular application and social context. However, the anti-theory sentiments are echoed not only by 'non-academics' but also by those working within universities. With the 'push' in many UK psychology departments to be involved in grant bidding activity, this has tended to relegate the focus on theory and epistemology – which is a crucial foundation on which to build and further a psychogeographical psychological approach. Indeed, in my discussions with other colleagues, there is a sense that there isn't time to think about theory and there certainly isn't time to philosophise or to have time to generate new methodologies and frameworks. These are things that seemingly only PhD and postdoctoral students can now do. The 'real' work of academics in the United Kingdom these days is to bid for large amounts of money to the research councils and to write up the findings of research for publication in peer-reviewed academic journals and to provide summary reports to the councils.

The money, it seems, has more value than what the research is about or what the outputs and impacts of the studies should be. It is therefore unsurprising when we find that our undergraduate psychology students do not 'get' theory or where they do not see the point of it. Indeed, for many, as long as they can competently display that they can apply set methods to topics, then they do not need to know about the theory underpinning research. Such an approach clearly sets such students at a disadvantage, particularly in relation to critical and qualitative psychological research. Many students also have immense trouble getting their heads around the theoretical underpinnings of psychological research and why theory is important in doing qualitative and quantitative research. For example, in one edited collection of papers on psychogeography and counselling for an academic publisher, I was asked to remove the theoretical focus of the work from my proposed chapter. I couldn't bring myself to take out the theoretical underpinning to the chapter as I didn't want to make my work descriptive, and so a mutual agreement was made to withdraw my chapter. It seems sad that there is becoming such a reluctance to engage in theory in academia and that we need to essentially dumb down our writing even for academic audiences. There is a real need for theory to understand and critique the present order of things. What we do and how we live our lives are always underpinned by some sort of theoretical framework. Indeed, beyond academia, there appears to be an anti-theory sentiment that has carried itself across into the world of politics, the media and everyday life (Butler, 2021) – that we do not need experts, i.e. Trump. However, I would argue that there is a real need to consider how we theoretically build new approaches, practices and methodologies whether that be in academia or beyond. The theory 'void' brings me to my next critical argument, which centres on the reversal back to cognitivism and in considering what is 'left' in critical psychology.

The cognitive turn and what is 'left' of critical psychology?

In my experience as a PhD student in the late 1990s, there felt like there was much hope in critical psychological approaches and methodologies and their application to wider society. There were many centres of critical and community psychological research, particularly in the United Kingdom including in Bath, Bolton and Manchester (where I undertook my PhD). However, in recent years, there has been a disappearance of many of these critical and community psychological centres and a subsequent building up of cognitive psychological research centres, or what could be referred to as a cognitive 'tsunami' (Dalal, 2018). These decisions about research centre groups have often been made with the Research Excellence Framework in mind whereby all academics in psychology departments are required to submit academic papers and where papers with quantitative, cognitive and neuropsychological arguments are ranked more highly and thus have more 'legitimacy'. Thus, the qualitative and critical psychological research gets 'wiped out' by such tsunami tidal waves. Critical psychological research with distinct political focuses such as psychogeographical research thus becomes 'obscured' from view. This then raises the question as to whether it is still possible to be qualitative and critical psychological in psychology departments. There are indeed some spaces for critical research such as walking methodologies within the Culture and Social Psychology Centre at the Open University and at the Centre for Narrative Research (i.e. Burnett et al., 2004). However, in other disciplines such as human geography, cultural studies and sociology, psychogeography and interest in the theory and practice has more visibility and respectability. This then raises the question as to whether it is necessary to work in and/or beyond the disciplinary boundaries of psychology. This brings me therefore into the next subsection of this chapter in terms of considering the steps into and beyond psychology.

Next steps and the move in and beyond psychology

In previous work, Parker has invoked the argument of doing away with psychology, and he refers to this with the argument of 'outwith' psychology. I would broadly concur with such arguments and would want to make the case that we need to work in and beyond the discipline of psychology. As radical academics, activists and artists, we should be working across disciplinary and perspectival boundaries. In Fozooni's recent book (2020), he builds on Parker's arguments with the idea of what he refers to as 'postpsychology'. Fozooni's (2004) paper presented at the International Conference of Critical Psychology in Bath was titled 'Fuck Critical Psychology', which stands as a clear demarcation of his work from the critical psychology fraternity. Whilst I don't fully subscribe to that position, what I do take from that argument is to be critical of critical psychology and to ensure that I do research that works to enable radical social change in the spirit of the situationists and other Marxist individuals and groups. Critical psychology without an agenda of radical social change is neither critical nor political.

I want to return now back to the title of this book, *Psychogeography and Psychology: In and Beyond the Discipline*. During the process of writing this book, the title worked well to encapsulate the association that I wanted to make of psychogeography with psychology. That, psychogeography could be a part of the subject of psychology and could be done so in order to widen out the range of existing methods and approaches and also to consider 'changing the subject of psychology' in the vein of arguments borrowed from Henriques et al.'s (1984) book. However, in further consideration, psychogeography could also be considered as an approach and method beyond the discipline of psychology and as a subject in its own right. When Henriques et al. (1984) wrote their landmark text, *Changing the Subject: Psychology, Social Regulation and Social Subjectivity*, they did so in order to challenge the traditional approach to psychology of cognitivism and experimentation and they presented alternative and more critical foundations to the discipline with the contribution of psychoanalytic, feminist and discursive critical psychological approaches. The case should now be made for what comes after psychology and that we need a 'postpsychology' (Fozooni, 2020). Any critical work situated in the subject can now potentially become assimilated back into being yet another 'novel' apolitical method for psychologists to use. I have witnessed this in my own work where colleagues in psychology and neighbouring disciplines consider psychogeography as just a methodology and that it is just about walking-based interviews and is just another form of data collection. It could be argued then that psychogeography can be co-opted back into the university by it being understood only as a method or technique for psychologists to use. Such views overlook the radical and political reasons for the dérive and of other important concepts such as detournement, participatory creativity and psychogeography. Therefore, I make a case here for a continuation of the development of the psychogeographical approach in the discipline but where this can take us beyond psychology in order to connect with the context of the everyday. Situationists such as Debord (1970) and Vaneigem (1975) argued for a revolution of everyday life and arguably a revolution is still needed today. This brings me to the final subsection of this chapter, which is to consider the contribution of psychogeography in a post COVID-19 work and to conclude with what a post-'Chtcheglovian' formulary for a new urbanism could look like. I will remind readers what is meant by the Chtcheglovian Formulary for a new urbanism in the next subsection.

In the early days of the COVID-19 pandemic, there was some hope that we would move to more politically ethical, sustainable and environmentally conscious ways of living. However, more recently, the return to 'normality' is met with moving back to how things are and thus with the neoliberal mode of societal organisation. This is a missed opportunity though there is still plenty that can be done using methods and practices such as psychogeography and post situationist theory. The configuration of a psychogeographical approach must adapt to the challenges of the world as it is today. As I have argued in this book previously, psychogeography does not need to necessarily 'stay' with psychology as it can exist within and across many academic disciplines as well as be of relevance to artists and activists. Psychogeography can be used to overturn, disrupt and consider new ways of doing psychology as well as new ways of thinking and being in the social world.

What has not been addressed in this book so far is the role of digitisation in psychogeographical inquiry. This is an area that I am keen to explore in the aftermath of this book – particularly in terms of how people navigate the internet and how the 'flattened' space of the web enables us to orient ourselves online. The tech companies such as Google, Amazon and eBay are keen for people to navigate in specific ways to their websites and much of the web is designed to lead us back to them. Further, companies such as Apple build 'walls' around their systems so that their users do not stray beyond Apple software and hardware. These companies do not want us to wander beyond their products and systems. Their strategies thus run counter to situationist and psychogeographical tactics of detournement, the derive and diversion though they do also draw on such techniques to keep us within their walled gardens. Open-source software and systems seem to be a key way to subvert the walled gardens and the linear routes through which the big tech companies want us to move in and around. During the COVID-19 pandemic, we have seen an increased use of technology to keep people connected with each other (i.e. Teams, Zoom, etc.) as well as people relying much more so on services and goods through companies such as Amazon and the big supermarkets. Arguably then, there is an increased digitisation of everyday life and social spaces, and thus, further psychogeographical research would be useful to explore this area.

Secondly, psychogeography should not just be the preserve of university students and scholars, and so it must be 'given away' to anyone who has interest and wishes to embark on doing research and activism using such methods and practices. Taking a position as a 'scholar activist' is a key important strategic standpoint to take, and it is worthwhile to conduct work that straddles the boundaries of academia, art and activism. Such work must be done to begin to enable social change in small ways. In Marx's (1847) classic text, *The Poverty of Philosophy* , he refers to the idea that people should take on a range of roles from fishing to cooking and cleaning rather than having a specialised role, which can lead to 'social alienation' and a lack of understanding of wider social systems and structures. Psychogeographical work can have value outside of universities, and therefore important work with community organisations and stakeholders can be done including arranging festivals, workshops, conferences, walks and other psychogeographical events. Indeed, within the North of England, there are several psychogeographical groups that are composed of artists, academics, activists and people from all walks of life and backgrounds such as the Leeds Psychogeography Group, the Huddersfield Psychogeographical Network and the Loiterers Resistance Movement. Such groups have organised a range of events including exhibitions, conferences and festivals in recent years. This work can be important to do in order to build connections with artists, activists and academics in working towards projects for social change. This work can also be useful in terms of community engagement and in developing arts-based research, as evidenced through work with the Hoot organisation and Huddersfield Art Gallery by Bridger et al. (2017). It is particularly pertinent to refer here to arguments raised by Hodgetts et al. (2014, 164), where they argue that, 'We need to embrace the long history in psychology of working in partnership with communities to challenge inequitable social structures and to affect change'. Psychogeographical research and practice enables its users to work in 'partnership with communities', and this can be done to question 'social structures' that may be 'inequitable' in order to begin to effect social changes. The focus of social change in relation to psychological research and practice seems to have been 'lost along the way' somewhat, and this is then the next point to flag as important in the development of psychogeographical research and practice.

Whilst psychogeographical work within psychology can effect change in turns of creating a spatial turn, a wider question is in relation to what social changes can be enabled beyond academic published work and academia. Colleagues such as McDonald et al. (2017, 7) argue that 'The aim of psychogeographical work is to promote more democratic, inclusive public spaces that transcend the narrow instrumental basis of most consumer spaces whose purpose is commodity production and consumption'. Arguably, psychogeographical work becomes commodified and recuperated through publication and through tenure of academics into universities where such individuals can be branded as 'methodologists'. However, it would be impossible to 'stand' completely outside of neoliberal systems and structures, and this raises a particular conundrum in terms of doing radical research in and beyond universities. Block (2007, 326) argues that critical psychologists need to 'work in concert with political allies to wage campaigns that will challenge Market Fundamentalism directly' and he refers to this as a form of 'public critical social psychology' (Block, 2007). McDonald et al. (2017) explain that psychogeography is one approach that can be considered as a 'decommodified' approach in psychology, which can be used to call in question the commodification of everyday life. In this work, I have discussed psychogeographical research conducted in areas such as Manchester City Centre after the IRA (Irish Republican Army) bombing. Indeed, since that work, there have been further terrorist attacks including the Manchester Arena bombing in 2017. Indeed, colleagues and psychogeographers in the Manchester area have attempted to consider these attacks in sensitive and considerate ways through organising discussions and events to bring people together. There is value in bringing together psychogeographers and various people from a range of backgrounds and disciplines not only to consider how to make sense of traumatic events such as terrorism attacks and other situations/events but also to consider how to imagine what the future might look like – utopian imaginings. The situationists' central argument was not to just study urbanism but also to provide a critique of urbanism and to overthrow capitalist society. The first part of their argument is achievable in drawing on situationism though the second part is rather more difficult. Creating social change is a lengthy and long drawn-out process. Enabling any change in a discipline such as psychology is, as I have realised, very hard to do because the discipline is so steeped in tradition and in adhering firmly to a 'scientific' viewpoint wedded heavily to positivism and empiricism. Many psychology colleagues whom I have worked with over the years simply do not understand qualitative methods and critical psychology. For many psychologists from a cognitive tradition, there is simply no need to understand about philosophy and history as they can conduct research and use quantitative methods to investigate hypotheses.

Doing psychogeographical work is arguably of use in terms of enabling people to think about: how environments make them feel, the effects of particular places and spaces, considering the extent to which such work can effect change and in terms of what personal and social changes are possible. As argued in previous work (Bridger et al., 2019), 'The psychogeographical "turn" is deployed to critique the consumer capitalist landscape and to build reflective awareness in communities about how neoliberal commodification impacts on our everyday lives'. The point of such work is to produce collective routes for action to take place in order to begin to work out how to change situations and society. There can be no fixed answers as to what change needs to occur and what should go in the place of neoliberal consumer capitalist spaces and places. The situationists did not attempt to answer such questions as they believed that people would come together to create change and to map out the future that they really wanted. Doing psychogeographical writing and walking does not in itself change anything, but it can change the ways in which we think about the social world and it can help us begin to envisage a world beyond a consumer capitalist order of things. Radical social change cannot in itself happen with just one person as it is something that takes many people to do. What would a world beyond a neoliberal consumer capitalist order of things look like? These are questions that are not easily answered and it would be impossible to do. Arguably, it is up to people themselves to come together to think of these questions and what the answers might be. We need to look at the 'cracks in the pavement' and see what alternatives there could be to the dominant order of things.

Some of the basic tenets of thought that the situationist grappled with from the mid-1950s to the late 1960s are still things that need to be fought for today. Though whilst the terrain may have changed somewhat, we still live under consumer capitalist conditions with great inequalities within society between the rich and the poor.

I hope that this book has provided some potential directions and the ways in which people can develop their own psychogeographical approaches. In the words of Portugese revolutionaries, 'a luta continua', which means 'the struggle continues'.

A reworking of Ivain Chtcheglov's 'Formulary for a new urbanism'

I conclude this book with a poetic reworking of Ivain Chtcheglov's (1958) 'Formulary for a new urbanism'. In previous published papers and book chapters, I have made the case that social change can only occur through people-led movements rather than political parties. I still believe that to be the case and consider that change beyond a consumer capitalist order of things is possible. But I want to finish this book with a case for poetry as being part of making these new realities come into being. One leading situationist Raoul Vaneigem (1967, n.p.) argued the following, 'This poetry is also radical theory embodied in action: the mortar binding tactics and revolutionary strategy; the high point of the great gamble on everyday life'. Here then I provide a reworking of Chtcheglov's text, which I hope may lead readers into considering their own ways of creating social change and in thinking about new types of psychologies both critical and post psychological:

Comrades, I am in the countryside near to the town of Huddersfield.

'WE ARE BORED' in the countryside, 'there is no longer any' God. Between the comings and goings of people wandering by, the situationists, democratic socialists and psychogeographers, they imagined a world beyond capitalism. Where are we now? 'We know how to' read and overturn the consumer 'signs' of society. We are bored in the countryside, we struggle to find meaning there and in the cities:

Huddersfield Leisure Centre
Amcor Meat Packing
Yorkshire Wildlife Park
Cohens Chemist
Huddersfield Parish Church
Masjid Riza
Salamander Fabrications Limited
IQ Games
Head of Steam
Coffee Evolution
Tesco
Premier Inn Huddersfield
Queensgate Market
Kirkgate

And the swimming pool in Slawit. And the police station just off Albion Street. The Huddersfield Royal Infirmary. The Clarion Court Hotel, Travelodge, the Huddersfield Hotel.

And the statue of Harold Wilson, once the leader of the Labour Party and founder of the Open University. This is Huddersfield.

The Sex Pistols played their last gig in Huddersfield. This town, once a ruler of the British reggae movement. A working-class town and home to the oldest Constituency Labour Party in the United Kingdom. The Hacienda isn't here, it is in Manchester. Once a music venue run by situationist inspired Tony Wilson. Now a block of flats – gentrified Manchester. Manchester after Marx and Engels. The Hacienda doesn't exist. The hacienda needs to be built again.

All places can be considered through psychogeographical perspectives. It isn't possible to move through environments without encountering memories and 'ghosts' from the past. The toppling of the Edward Coulson statue in Bristol, the Black Lives Matter movement, the history of colonialism and the British Empire. The British Tory Government, Johnson, Patel and English footballers Mings, Saka, Sancho and Rashford. Taking the knee considered as 'gesture politics'. Stoking the fires and English pride as banal nationalism. We still enter into closed landscapes where particular landmarks, sites and places draw us back to the past. Nigel Farage, Enoch Powell, Donald Trump and the Proud Boys 'Standing By' … a world beyond fascism and racism … is it possible?

All people shift from the 'emotionally alive past and the already dead future'.

We shouldn't 'prolong' this 'mechanistic' civilisation and its generic consumer capitalist architecture any longer as it can lead only to passitivity and non-inspiring forms of entertainment and ways of being.

Instead, new and changeable environments must be constructed …

Work at home, work at work, work as a consumer and buy more. Instead replace work with love, joy and pleasure over boredom and bureaucratic capitalism and consumption. Reconfigure, deconstruct, create new, subvert, interrupt, change and detourn all things, systems and society. Future architecture must be post situationist and should work to enacting new modulations of time, place and space. Architecture as a 'means of action' and for social change. The next civilisation must be EXPERIMENTAL, enjoyable and flexible to various ways of changing everyday life.

The coronavirus pandemic has swept through the world creating health crises whilst the spectre of the climate crisis looms ever closer with rising global temperatures, the melting of the ice caps, increased flooding risks and fires in wild moorland, forests and other areas. The environment and the climate at odds with the needs of capitalist economics and big business. With global lockdowns due to the pandemic, we have retreated back to our screens, to television, computers, tablets and phones. These technologies though enable us to remain connected with loved ones, friends, family and work colleagues. The big tech companies profit the most i.e. Amazon, Apple, Facebook, Google, Zoom, Microsoft, and so on. Consumable products and services. People 'hypnotised' by items on the sales and by the latest 'must have' smartphones, computers and 4K televisions. The spectacle locks us into place in front of our screens making it more difficult than ever to refuse the advertisements for new washing machines, televisions and cars. I buy therefore I am.

How to liberate ourselves from materialism and do we need to? Global poverty and austerity continues, whilst the rich get richer and the very rich are able to conduct missions to fly into space – Branson, Bezos and Musk. Do not believe what the voice-over tells you in the Lloyds Bank television advertisement. The banks are not your friends.

It is not simply a choice for young people to choose revolution or convenience. Fear makes everyone focus on the need to get a good job, choose a course that will be well-paid and which will secure employment. The screws are tightened, with a narrowing of choices for young and old.

Situations must be constructed, which can lead to the development of new civilisations. On Earth, on Mars with Musk or elsewhere. Play rather than banalisation and bureaucracy.

Bauhaus, Constant, Jorn, Chtcheglov, Wark, Richardson, Debord, Bollinger. These people and others providing the blueprints for post situationist architecture, forms of living and new worlds.

New visions of time, place and space – these things form the theoretical foundations for future worlds. We must experiment with patterns of behaviour and thinking until the founding of new societies and civilisations.

'Everyone will live in their own personal "cathedral". There will be rooms more conducive to dreams than any other drug, and houses where one cannot help but love'.

Towns, cities and the countryside could be a random assemblage of buildings with each area being designed to elicit a range of emotional expressions. The areas could be as follows: living area (peoples' homes), education (schools, universities), useful area (hospitals, DIY), entertainment (cinema, skating, etc) and so on.

'The main activity of the inhabitants will be CONTINUOUS DRIFTING. The changing of landscapes from one hour to the next will result in total disorientation ....'.

Places should be constructed to enable 'free play' (Chtcheglov, 1958, n.p.). By this, it is not simply meant as places such as the gambling venues in Las Vegas and Monaco, but rather as areas that facilitate 'avante-garde activities and productions'.

Poetry is somewhere and everywhere. It lives in books, the arts and our everyday lives. When repressed, it resurfaces everywhere from street walls, to carnivals, in song and all places and spaces. Poetry as lived, a visceral force for change, disobeying the rules of convention and order. Spontaneity, change, new words and worlds.

What is a formulary for a new urbanism? The formulary must be constructed. Write it and then do put it into practice. Revolutions in psychology and revolutions in everyday life. Go out into the world and create social change.

References

Block, F. (2007). Confronting market fundamentalism: Doing "public economic sociology". *Socio-Economic Review*, 5(2), 326–334. Retrieved from the Cite Seer X website: https://citeseerx.ist.psu.edu/viewdoc/download?doi=10.1.1.538.2969&rep=rep1&type=pdf

Bridger, A.J., Emmanouil, S., & Lawthom, R. (2017). trace.space: A psychogeographical community project with members of an arts and health organisation. *Qualitative Research in Psychology*, 14(1), 42–61. https://doi.org/10.1080/14780887.2016.1219799

Bridger, A.J., Emmanouil, S., & Lawthom, R. (2019). The psychogeographical turn in applied social psychology. In K. O'Doherty & D. Hodgetts (Eds.), *The sage handbook of applied social psychology* (pp. 515–529). London: Sage.

Burnett, J., Cudworth, E., & Tamboukou, M. (2004). Women on dérive: Autobiographical explorations of lived spaces. In *Women and Geography Study Group, Geography and Gender Reconsidered*. CD-ROM, August: 118–141.

Butler, J. (2021). "We need to rethink the category of woman". Gleeson, J. *The Guardian*. September 7, 2021. www.theguardian.com/lifeandstyle/2021/sep/07/judith-butler-interview-gender

Chtcheglov, I. (1958). *Formulary for a new urbanism*. Retrieved from the Situationist International website: www.cddc.vt.edu/sionline/presitu/formulary.html

Dalal, F. (2018). *CBT: The cognitive behavioural tsunami*. London: Routledge.

Debord, G. (1970). *The society of the spectacle*. London: Black and Red.

Debord, G. (2010). *Comments on the society of the spectacle*. London: Verso.

Fozooni, B. (2004). Fuck critical psychology! *International Conference of Critical Psychology*, University of Bath.

Fozooni, B. (2020). *Psychology, humour and class: A critique of contemporary class*. London: Routledge.

Freeman, J. (1972). *The tyranny of structurelessness*. Retrieved from the Jo Freeman website: www.jofreeman.com/joreen/tyranny.htm

Henriques, J., Hollway, W., Urwin, C., Venn, C., & Walkerdine, V. (1984). *Changing the subject: Psychology, social regulation and social subjectivity*. London: Routledge.

Hodgetts, D., Stolte, O., & Groot, S. (2014). Towards a relationally and action-orientated applied social psychology of homelessness. *Social and Personality Psychology Compass*, 8(4), 156–164. https://doi.org/10.1111/spc3.12096

Marx, K. (1847). *The poverty of philosophy*. Paris and Brussels: Progress Publishers. Retrieved from the Marxist Archive website: www.marxists.org/archive/marx/works/1847/poverty-philosophy/index.htm

McDonald, M., Bridger, A.J., Wearing, S.L., & Ponting, J. (2017). Consumer spaces as political spaces: A critical review of social, environmental and psychogeographical research. *Social and Personality Psychology Compass*, 11(7). https://doi.org/10.1111/spc3.12325

Parker, I. (2007). *Revolution in psychology: From alienation to emancipation*. London: Pluto Press.

Parker, I. (2015). *Psychology after the crisis: Scientific paradigms and political debate*. London: Routledge.

Plant, S. (1992). *The most radical gesture: The situationist international in a post-modern age*. London: Routledge.

Rose, M. (2015). Confessions of an Anarcho-Flâneuse or psychogeography the Mancunian Way. In T. Richardson (Ed.), *Walking inside out: Contemporary British psychogeography* (pp. 147–164). London: Roman and Littlefield.

Vaneigem, R. (1967). *The revolution of everyday life*. Retrieved from the Nothingness website: http://library.nothingness.org/articles/SI/en/pub_contents/5

Vaneigem, R. (1975). *The revolution of everyday life*. London: Practical Paradise.

INDEX